The Deeds
of the Franks and Other
Jerusalem-Bound Pilgrims

The Earliest Chronicle of the First Crusades

Edited and Translated
by
Nirmal Dass

ROWMAN & LITTLEFIELD PUBLISHERS, INC.
Lanham • Boulder • New York • Toronto • Plymouth, UK

Published by Rowman & Littlefield Publishers, Inc.
A wholly owned subsidary of The Rowman & Littlefield Publishing Group, Inc.
4501 Forbes Boulevard, Suite 200, Lanham, Maryland 20706
http://www.rowmanlittlefield.com

Estover Road, Plymouth PL6 7PY, United Kingdom

British Library Cataloguing in Publication Information Available

Library of Congress Cataloging-in-Publication Data

Gesta Francorum et aliorum Hierosolymitanorum. English.
   The deeds of the Franks and other Jerusalem-bound pilgrims : the earliest
chronicle of the first crusades / edited and translated by Nirmal Dass.
   p. cm.
   Summary: "This new translation offers a faithful yet accessible English-
language rendering of the twelfth-century Gesta Francorum et aliorum
Hierosolomitanorum, the earliest known Latin account of the First Crusade. The
exemplar for all later histories and retellings of the First Crusade, it is filled with
vivid descriptions of the hardships suffered by the crusaders, with deeds of personal
heroism, with courtly intrigues, with betrayal and cowardice, and with a relentless
faith that would see the attainment of the desired goal: the capture of Jerusalem
by the crusaders in 1095. It is also a sweeping tale that swiftly moves from the first
preaching of the crusade by Pope Urban II, to the ragtag and ultimately doomed
effort of the popular People's Crusade, and then to the more disciplined and
concerted campaign by the French and Norman nobility that led to the conquest
of the Holy Land by the crusaders. Based on the latest scholarly research, including
a substantive introduction that explores the questions surrounding the Gesta and
that sets it in its historical context, this definitive translation will bring the First
Crusade and its era to life for all readers" —Provided by publisher.
   Includes bibliographical references and index.
   ISBN 978-1-4422-0497-3 (hardback) — ISBN 978-1-4422-0498-0
(paperback) — ISBN 978-1-4422-0499-7 (electronic)
   1. Crusades—First, 1096–1099. I. Dass, Nirmal, 1962– II. Title.
   D161.1.G413 2011
   956'.014—dc23   2011022885

Printed in the United
States of America

Contents

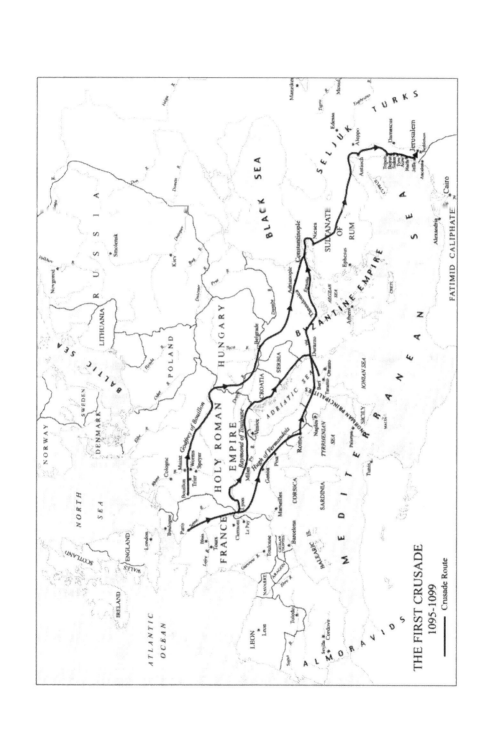

THE FIRST CRUSADE
1095-1099

—— Crusade Route

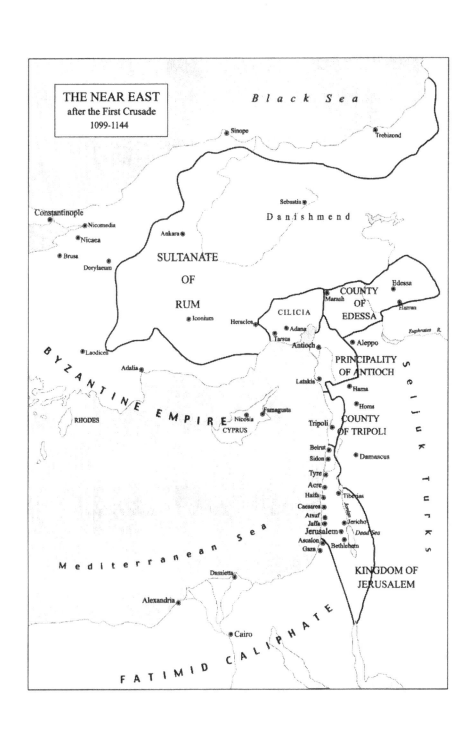

THE NEAR EAST
after the First Crusade
1099-1144

Black Sea

Sinope

Trebizond

Constantinople

Nicomedia

Nicaea

Brusa

Dorylaeum

Sebastia

D a n i s h m e n d

Ankara

SULTANATE

OF

RUM

Iconium

Heraclea

CILICIA

Adana

Tarsus

Marash

COUNTY

OF

EDESSA

Edessa

Harran

Euphrates R.

Laodicea

Adalia

Antioch

Aleppo

PRINCIPALITY

OF ANTIOCH

B Y Z A N T I N E   E M P I R E

RHODES

Nicosia

Famagusta

CYPRUS

Latakia

Hama

Homs

COUNTY

OF TRIPOLI

S e l j u k   T u r k s

Tripoli

Beirut

Sidon

Damascus

Tyre

Acre

Haifa

Tiberias

Caesarea

Atsuf

Jordan

Jaffa

Jericho

Jerusalem

Dead Sea

Ascalon

Bethlehem

Gaza

KINGDOM OF

JERUSALEM

M e d i t e r r a n e a n   S e a

Damietta

Alexandria

Cairo

F A T I M I D   C A L I P H A T E

Introduction

AUTHORSHIP

The Gesta Francorum et aliorum Hierosolimitanorum (the *Gesta*), or "the deeds of the Franks and other Jerusalemites," is the primal source for the First Crusade.[1] The various other extant chronicles of this crusade chiefly depend upon it for episodic and narrative structure, although the *Gesta's* primacy has often been questioned.[2] The title of the work has been given to it from the earliest manuscript tradition, and the Latin term *Hierosolimitanorum*, or "of the *Jerusalemites*," in the title of the work points to a medieval practice of associating pilgrims with the holy place they were going to visit. Thus, the crusaders were Jerusalemites because they were pilgrims on their way to the Holy Sepulcher (the tomb in which Jesus was buried) in Jerusalem. The *Gesta* is an anonymous work; nor can it be clearly ascertained where it might have been written. Paleographic evidence firmly suggests a European origin; handwriting practiced in the Latin Near East was markedly different.[3] The manuscripts also suggest a date around the first half of the twelfth century—well within living memory of the various events described in the *Gesta*. If an original version of the *Gesta* existed in Jerusalem, it has not survived; we only have European copies of it. The fact that some sort of a book about the First Crusade might have existed in Jerusalem is certain, since a visitor there states that he saw such a little book, a *libellus*, in 1101. The visitor's name was Ekkehard of Aura, the famous chronicler, and his testimony is important in helping us understand how the *Gesta* came to exist in its present form.[4]

When dealing with a source such as the *Gesta*, two important questions immediately come to mind: Who wrote it? And is it an eyewitness account? Both questions are connected, since authorship suggests trustworthiness to the modern reader. If the authority of the author is missing, then the modern reader may well question the claims made in the book itself, since the modern world puts a great deal of confidence in individualized knowledge. Thus, in the present age it is often experts who write books, and readers turn to these books because of that authorial expertise.

Things were different in the Middle Ages. The authority of books came not from individual expertise but from tradition, and books were written in order to elaborate (but not change) that tradition. Thus, a book of history arose from, participated in, and elaborated on, the tradition of historiography that included classical sources—but more importantly it included the Bible. In fact, writing history without the Bible was unimaginable in the Middle Ages. And this medieval tradition of history was interested in providing the panoramic view rather than the individualized, particular one, because history was not about interpreting the actions of men, but about understanding the workings of God in human affairs. And so the questions—who wrote the *Gesta*, and is it an eyewitness account—are ultimately unimportant, because the *Gesta* is trying to relate not the experiences dependent upon personal expertise, but upon the tradition of history in the medieval world—the *Gesta* wants to provide a panoramic view of the First Crusade in order to make it obvious that this event is just one more episode in God's grand scheme of redemption for humankind.

However, this has not stopped scholars from trying to guess who the author of the *Gesta* might have been. And over the years, three distinct answers have been provided for the question, who wrote the *Gesta*?

The first answer, which is the oldest,[5] sees the author as the younger son of a southern Italian nobleman, and therefore a Norman, who was being trained to become a priest, but when the crusade was announced, he dropped everything and became a crusader and fought all the way to Jerusalem. As he fought, he sat down and faithfully wrote down what he did and saw; and so he is giving us a firsthand, eyewitness account of what exactly happened. He reached Jerusalem, took part in its capture, and then wrote about it. Since the purpose of the entire First Crusade was the capture of Jerusalem, this Norman author wraps up his book with this event. It is this book that we now call the *Gesta*. And, as for that little book that Ekkehard saw, this first answer suggests that it was nothing other than the account written by the Norman knight. This answer is weak, if not entirely wrong. Nowhere in the *Gesta* is there a specific or even a vague indication that the author is a younger son of some noble family. Nor is there any hint of evidence that the author is from southern Italy and a Norman. And there is no mention at all that the author interrupted his training for the priesthood to become a fighting crusader. As for the idea that the *Gesta* is an eyewitness account, again, nothing at all in the work would lead to that conclusion. Therefore, this first answer really is misleading and incorrect.

The second answer rigorously critiques the first one,[6] correctly pointing out that nothing in the *Gesta* points to any notion of one specific author. Instead of one author, the second answer posits the *Gesta* as the work of a scriptorium, of monks sifting through various narratives of the First Crusade and then writing the *Gesta* based upon their research. This explains why there are so many instances of "misreadings" and of names being mixed up. Surely the author of a firsthand account would have made sure that he got the names right. Thus, this second answer suggests that the *Gesta* is not an eyewitness account at all but is based upon a compilation of "field reports," that is, short, firsthand experiences of various crusaders.[7] These reports would then have been collated into a little book of sorts, and it was this book that Ekkehard saw; it was not the "real" version of the *Gesta* at all, since that had not yet been written. There is much to recommend this second answer because it recognizes that the medieval historian was concerned not with individual authorship but with the tradition of doing history to explicate God's grand plan for humanity—each historical event pointed to the verity of that plan. And also importantly this answer understands that the writing of a book in the Middle Ages was a collective effort and not an individual one.

The third answer is skeptical about the implications of the second one, namely the emphasis on authorship, whether individual or collective.[8] In its place, it sees the *Gesta* as a purely literary endeavor and not at all the record of actual experience of one individual or many; nor can it even be the objective observation of an observer of the First Crusade, since both these ideas at once suggest authorial expertise and intent. Rather, this third answer advises that the *Gesta* must be read in the context of medieval historiography, which privileges divine inspiration (proper understanding) over direct observation, and therefore the question of authorship is unimportant. This answer does not consider Ekkehard's testimony. There is a great deal of merit to this third answer, because it stresses the role of tradition in the Middle Ages. However, it is too eager to abandon the insights offered by the second answer. The best way to begin understanding the issue of authorship is to consider a fourth possibility—that the manuscript tradition indeed suggests a clear authorship.

Firstly, it is reasonable to assume that the real "author" of the work was an institution. It was the "production team" of a scriptorium that produced the book known as the *Gesta*. This explains the various instances of misreadings, especially of names, and the many occasions when the narrative is unclear and the events fuzzy, because these are examples of "editorial" uncertainty and "educated guesses." But if an institution was involved, why is the language of the *Gesta* rough and unrefined? For it was the "barbaric Latin" (*Latina-barbara*) of the original that annoyed Baudri de Bourgueil and Guibert of Nogent so much that they both launched into rewriting the *Gesta* to give it a more polished and refined finish.[9]

This question of language is important. Is the rough Latin of the *Gesta* reflective of ordinary speech, used by gruff soldiers, although such soldiers would have spoken the vernacular of their day, such as Norman French, Old French, Provençal, or medieval Italian, depending on their origin? Did a monkish scribe translate what these soldiers told him; and since he had to get everything down in a hurry, he simply carried into Latin the rough speech habits of his soldier-narrators? Or did these same soldiers write their reports in the vernacular, which were then translated into Latin? The answer to all three questions is, likely not. Certainly, the "barbaric Latin" does seem to give the *Gesta* an air of authenticity: We are listening in on a soldier speaking of his experiences in the "war." But this is precisely the point—the "barbaric Latin" is literary style; the Latin is constructed to sound like common twelfth-century speech. The unrefined diction and hurried syntax is an act of the imagination, an attempt to capture the speech patterns of soldiers, very much like the "imagined" speech of Muslims in the *Gesta*, which is always overly contrived and at times outlandish. And because we have no surviving vernacular sources in which we encounter a non-Latin version of the *Gesta*, the conclusion is obvious— the *Gesta* is not a translation of a non-Latin source or sources but a composition uniquely in Latin. The use of the pronouns *I, us*, and *we* is not any proof of an eyewitness account; it is merely a matter of point of view— "us" against "them." These pronouns led to the erroneous view that the *Gesta* was a firsthand, eye-witness account. But great care must be taken with such easy conclusions, since point of view is, again, a matter of literary style. Further, the use of the pronoun *I* in the *Gesta* simply suggests that the authors of the work are using the "field notes" of someone who wrote down what he knew.

And the testimony of Ekkehard of Aura is also important in this regard, because he does attest to seeing a "little book," and it is important to note the Latin term he uses to describe it—*libellus*, "little book," which means that the source was not a substantial tome of crusade history. Likely it was no more than a chronology and summary of the main events that happened over the four-year period of the First Crusade, and perhaps it also included the names of important people and a brief episodic "marker" of what they did—so-and-so did this and that at such a place and at such a day, month, or year. This *libellus* would have been written by a cleric in Latin, since Ekkehard understood it—Ekkehard was a German, and it is unlikely that he would have read Old French. More importantly, if the little book were in Old French, Ekkehard would have modified *libellus* to make clear that he had before him a non-Latin source, a *libellus vulgaris*, "a little book in the vernacular." In the absence of such a description, *libellus* by itself can only readily be taken to mean a little book in Latin. And perhaps there were several such "little books" in circulation throughout Europe in the years following the capture of Jerusalem in 1099. The authors of the *Gesta* perhaps used one or more such versions to construct and write their own narrative.

However, it appears that the chronologies the authors of the *Gesta* possessed were uneven, because their finished work, rather curiously, spends a lot of time describing the siege and conquest of Antioch. But the siege and conquest of Jerusalem—which one might imagine would be the highlight, since the entire First Crusade was constructed around such an event—gets short shrift. This can only be explained by the suggestion that the authors used sources that were either uneven or incomplete.

The earliest manuscript of the *Gesta* likely gives us the very names of the authors of this work; in other words, there is evidence of a clear authorship. At the very end of the Vatican manuscript *Reginensis latini 641*, and tucked away, almost surreptitiously, at the bottom of folio 45, are two lines that give the names of four men. The handwriting is certainly from the first half of the twelfth century, the very era of the *Gesta*'s composition. In Latin, these two lines read *Petrus clericus de Mirabea. Wilelmus clericus de Vosaillia. Gauterea de Funfreide laicus. Johannes de Gelis laicus.* In English, "Peter, the clerk of Mirabeau. William, the clerk of Vosailles. Walter of Fontfroide, layman. John of Gélis, layman." The four names appear without explanation, but do belong to the twelfth century. Here, it seems, is the "production team" of a scriptorium, which hammered out the narrative of the *Gesta*. These names cannot be signatures, nor can they be the names of the owners of the manuscript; such methods of self-identity or marking of books were unknown at this time. Therefore, it is very likely that the clerks Peter from Mirabeau and William from Vosailles, and the laymen Walter from Fontfroide and John from Gélis together wrote the *Gesta*.

THE LANGUAGE OF THE *GESTA*

The Latin employed in the *Gesta* is devoid of ornamentation, besides being economical and precise. The "editorial decision" seems to be to tell the story in a style and tone that would fit the subject matter—war and the life of soldiers on campaign. This is not to say that the *Gesta* is ignorant of literary effects. For example, the lengthy speech by Curbaram's mother is an elegant homily on the divine destiny of Christians, which is further strengthened by Curbaram's naïve questions about the nature of the men he is about to fight. Curbaram is the leader of all the Muslim forces who fight against the crusaders in the *Gesta*.

Further, it had been previously assumed that the pared-down language of the *Gesta* is reflective of the author's station—a fighting knight with a rudimentary grasp of Latin. However, it makes better sense to see the language of the *Gesta* as indicative of stylistic choices—to capture the simple, straightforward speech of soldiers. As a result, the Latin of the *Gesta* is very close to the vernacular of the day (the emerging French and Italian), which would have been the common speech of the crusaders. Thus, for example, the preposition *de* ("from") is used instead of *ex* (more typical of Latin), the gerund or the infinitive is replaced by the present participle, and there is a regular use of vernacular terms, such as, *burgus* for "suburb," *papilio* for "pavilion," and *azule* for "a piece of cloth." This is an attempt to capture the common, living speech of the crusader on the ground.

THE MANUSCRIPT TRADITION

The *Gesta* exists in seven extant manuscripts; and given the relationship that they exhibit one to another, they have been arranged into three different groups. The first group is the earliest and comprises the parchment Vatican manuscript, in folio, *Reginensis latini 572*, which once belonged to the French antiquarian Paul Petau (1568–1614) and which dates from the first half of the twelfth century. Next is the *Vatican MS Reginensis latini 641*, which likely dates from the later part of the twelfth century; it was once owned by Cardinal Alain de Coëtivy (1407–1474), who was the bishop of Avignon. Lastly, there is the *Madrid, Biblioteca Nacional E.e. 103 (9783)*, a parchment manuscript in quarto, which dates from the early part of the fourteenth century; it once belonged to the Marquis of Valleron, Joseph Louis Dominique de Cambis (1706–1772).

In content, all three manuscripts are similar in that they contain the *Gesta*, the description of the holy places in Jerusalem, a Mass in veneration of the Holy Sepulcher, and the dimensions of the Holy Sepulcher. In addition, *Reginensis latini 572* contains a quatrain in praise of Bohemond, and several folios have been added at the end, which include a letter by Oliver of Cologne (obit 1227), describing the siege of Damietta in 1219, during the Fifth Crusade. *Reginensis latini 641* has a quire missing, for at the bottom of folio 32 verso is found the note, of fourteenth-century orthography, *Hic deficit quaternio* ("here a quire is missing"). This manuscript also contains subtle changes, the purpose of which is to show Robert Curthose, the duke of Normandy, and one of the leaders of the crusaders, in a good light.

The language in the three manuscripts is also very similar in that it is unrefined and often betrays Germanic characteristics; for example, *nichil* for *nihil* ("nothing"); *sepulchrum* for *sepulcrum* ("sepulcher"), where the *ch* is guttural; or the term *Northmanni* for Normans, instead of the more Latinate *Normanni*. Plus, the Latin has typical medieval traits, such as the simplification of the diphthongs *oe* and *ae* into *e*, and the frequent omission of the initial *h*.

The second group comprises four manuscripts, and all of them are versions of *Reginensis latini 641*, with improvements and refinement of the Latin. Two of these are of English provenance. The first is a parchment manuscript dating from the late twelfth century, which was in the abbey of Barlings in Lincolnshire. It came into the possession of Antonio Agustín y Albanell (1516–1586), and from his library it came into the Real Biblioteca de San Lorenzo de El Escorial, where it is now housed as *D.III.ii*; it is bound with a collection of the lives of saints. On the title page, someone has jokingly written *Sutorii sive potius incerti Itinerarium Hierosolymorum*, that is, "The shoemakers, or the unknown Jerusalem Itinerary." The second manuscript of English provenance is in the Berlin Staatsbibliothek, referenced as *Latein 4o 503*. It dates from the thirteenth century and originally belonged to the priory of Kenilworth, in England. It was in the collection of Arthur Cowper Ranyard (1845–1894), the English astronomer. The manuscript is badly damaged, with several leaves missing. The third manuscript of this group is in Cambridge, Gonville and Caius College, reference number *162/83*. It dates from the thirteenth century or perhaps the fourteenth. The fourth manuscript is known as Cambridge, Corpus Christi College *281* and is an abbreviated version of the *Gesta*. It also tends to favor Duke Robert Curthose and places him at the head of each list of princes given in the work.

There is also somewhat of a mystery in the entire manuscript tradition in that the very first printed edition of the *Gesta* by Jacques Bongars (1546–1612), published in 1611 as *Gesta Dei per Francos* ("the deeds of God through the Franks"), was based upon two manuscripts. One belonged to Paul Petau (the *Reginensis latini 572*) and the other to William Camden (1551–1623), the great English historian. It is not certain which manuscript Camden possessed; Bongars states that it ended with the words *Explicit via bona* ("here the good way ends"). It may well have been another account of the First Crusade that has not survived. However, the title chosen by Bongars deserves comment in that it emphasizes the medieval notion of history—God actively involved in history in order to accomplish His great salvific plan. This also is the concern of medieval historiography, as previously mentioned, and indeed therefore of the entire *Gesta*, grounded as it is in the understanding that life is a sacred process toward a final, heavenly goal. Hence the journey toward Jerusalem is also everyman's path (and that certainly hard-won) through life and into a state of redemption.

THE STRUCTURE OF THE *GESTA*

The entire *Gesta* runs though ten narratives, or books, a division found in the earliest manuscripts. Thus, the first narrative proceeds up to the battle of Vardar. The second narrative ends with the capture of Nicaea; the third includes the battle of Dorylaeum; the fourth describes the march down to Antioch; the fifth, sixth, seventh, and eighth narratives are concerned with the siege of Antioch; the ninth deals with the Turkish counterattack at Antioch. The tenth, and the final, narrative deals with the deliverance of Antioch, the victory at Ascalon, and the taking of Jerusalem. All the narratives, with the exception of three and eight, end with a doxology, and such a conclusion further grounds the *Gesta* in sacred history.

The initial part of the first narrative comprises the preaching of the crusade by Pope Urban II and Peter the Hermit and the ensuing "People's Crusade" led by Peter the Hermit and Walter Sans-Avoir. After the slaughter at Civetot, the first narrative takes up the story of the assemblage and the journeys of the various leaders that made up the second part of the First Crusade, which has come to be known as the Princes' Crusade. It is also near the end of the initial narrative that the pronoun *we* is first used, which is an important stylistic indicator of a strongly partisan narrative from here on in—the narrative is built around the deeds of these princes. The remaining nine narratives move geographically eastward into present-day Turkey and then southward into what is now Lebanon, Syria, and Israel. As well, the *Gesta* is a mixture of historical fact and imaginative fancy. Details about the "deeds of the Franks" are grounded in sacred history, while the deeds of the Turks are grounded in speculative fantasy; they are thoroughly visualized as pagans who operate on a logic that is entirely contrary to the logic of the Christian world, and therefore the Turks, as pagans, reside outside the pale of sacred history.

The *Gesta* is uneven in that it is fuzzy about the early beginnings of the First Crusade and especially the People's Crusade, and it confuses some of the names of the lords involved in the Princes' Crusade. Also, it handles the intricacies of Byzantine politics clumsily so that the motivations of the emperor, Alexius I Comnenus, and the various lords are somewhat of a puzzle. However, with the march eastward from Constantinople, the account becomes more cohesive as the crusaders make their way toward the Holy Sepulcher in Jerusalem. Indeed, once the crusaders leave behind the labyrinth of Byzantine politics, their "job" is simple and straightforward—head to Jerusalem. And here the geographical details are precise and give a sweeping quality to the account as the crusader army, known as the "host,"[10] encounters the Turks at various points in their "pilgrimage" to Jerusalem. The mind-set of the Muslim Turks is also exotically imagined, although typically they are portrayed as true pagans who believe in many gods and worship idols (something that Muslims, of course, do not do). After the capture of Antioch the story begins to falter. The battle of Ascalon is hastily described, while the capture of Jerusalem seems little more than a sideshow, especially when compared to the high drama of the siege of Antioch and the taking of that city.

This imbalance in the *Gesta* suggests that the material available to the authors was uneven or incomplete, as indicated earlier. For example, six of the ten narratives are about Antioch. And when it comes to the battle of Ascalon and the taking of Jerusalem, the details that the authors possess are sketchy at best and rather ad hoc. It is as if the authors are on very unsure ground; the earlier confidence in the process of storytelling is gone. It has been replaced by a rapid summary of the main points and then a hurried conclusion. Perhaps it is for this reason that the manuscript tradition places at the end of the tenth narrative an itinerary of Jerusalem, a sort of traveler's guidebook of what to see in that city. And then to emphasize the purpose of the entire First Crusade, the prayers of a Mass that might well have been said at the Holy Sepulcher in 1099 are included. And then there is an interesting, though repetitive, quatrain in praise of Bohemond, the lord of the Sicilian-Norman contingent of crusaders, which is rather odd, since he is not the central character of the *Gesta*. Perhaps this quatrain was found in one of the sources that focused on the deeds of Bohemond, just as some accounts emphasized the role of Duke Robert Curthose of Normandy.

THE *GESTA* AND HISTORY

The *Gesta* tells the story of the First Crusade by continually shifting locales and therefore contexts. The narrative has a sweeping quality as it moves from Italy to France to Germany and then eastward toward Constantinople and Anatolia, or modern-day Turkey, and then south into what is now the state of Israel. These involve the reader with different histories, cultures, and geographical locations, and by doing so, the *Gesta* allows for a reconsideration of questions that lie at the very heart of the chronicle. What was a "crusade"? What were the conditions that brought about the First Crusade? And why did anyone want to become a "crusader"?

The term *crusade* is not medieval and only came to be used in English well into the sixteenth century, at which time it meant "crossed," or "being marked by the cross." The term does, however, focus on the sign that the medieval participants wore on or over their clothes, namely a cross, which identified them as particular types of pilgrims—those heading to Jerusalem. A modern example of this practice of marking a pilgrim is the scallop shell emblem that designates pilgrims walking the Way of St. James to the cathedral of Santiago de Compostela in Spain.

Thus, what is now termed as a *crusade* was called a pilgrimage in the medieval period. And when Pope Urban II set the First Crusade in motion, he called for pilgrims who would take a holy vow to head out to Jerusalem and once there do everything they could to free the Holy Sepulcher (the tomb of Jesus) from Turkish control. Unlike all other pilgrimages, however, this one had a special feature—it would be an armed one, in which the pilgrims would also have to fight those who might resist this act of liberation. The pilgrims would be the "soldiers of Saint Peter." But because it nevertheless was a pilgrimage, spiritual benefits, to compensate for this effort, were made available to the participants by Urban II.

Thus, on November 27, 1095, at the Council of Clermont, Pope Urban II preached the first of such armed pilgrimages, or the First Crusade. No exact text of his message survives, but the gist of what he said can be surmised from the various sources that reported the event: He called for a threefold effort of liberation—to free the Christians of the Middle East from humiliating Muslim rule, to restore dignity and glory to the Christian city of Byzantium, which was facing constant harassment from the Turks, and to free Jerusalem, the city of Christ, from Muslim possession. The power of his message was such that those assembled cried out in one voice, "God wills it! God wills it!"[11]

What was the context of this message, or what were the conditions that led to such an armed pilgrimage? Firstly, there was the emergence and reformulation of Western Europe after the meltdown of the Carolingian empire by the end of the tenth century. Secondly, there was Church reform and the rise of the papacy, both of which began in earnest in the eleventh century. Thirdly, there was the rapid establishment of the Seljuq Turkish Empire in the Middle East and Central Asia in the latter part of the eleventh century. And fourthly, there was the intricacy of the Byzantine world, especially as it sought to deal with the threat posed by the Turks who had successfully stripped away large parts of its territory.

By the time Urban II delivered his sermon at Clermont, Western Europe had undergone an entire revolution, politically, religiously, economically, and culturally. Until the end of the ninth century, most of Western Europe had functioned as a centralized unit in the form of the Carolingian Empire. But the success of its founder (Charlemagne) could not be repeated or maintained by his descendants, so that central authority completely broke down and ushered in a lengthy period of internecine warfare as one son of Charlemagne fought another for total authority. The result was political and economic chaos—and perhaps because of this chaos, this era also experienced countless devastating raids by the Vikings and then later by the marauding Magyars, which drained off precious wealth of both Church and state and also destroyed the lives of ordinary people.[12] Large tracts of land that had once been cultivated were abandoned for fear of the Vikings, and more and more people began to congregate around the castle of the lord to seek his protection. By doing so, they established the system of manorialism, in which the peasants got security in exchange for cultivating the local lord's land. Typically a field was divided into equal strips, some for the lord and some to feed the peasant and his family.[13]

The lack of centralized authority allowed governors to take possession of the various territories that they once managed for the Carolingian rulers, thereby carving their own personal principalities and dukedoms. Often these petty lords formed larger units for added protection and strength by pledging allegiance to one another; the lord that had the most territory often became the supreme authority figure in this relationship of obligations, of "feudalism," as it is commonly called. Thus, the humblest farmer to the highest lord owed allegiance to someone more powerful than he. Such interdependence also ensured that a small disagreement between two lords easily involved all their clients and vassals as well, which meant that both the tenth and eleventh centuries were very violent ones, especially for the ordinary person.[14]

But this ordinary person also now had a voice, because of the manorial system. Since people now lived together, they had a greater economic impact. Thus, these people began to object to the violence perpetrated by the lords upon them—and they demanded change. A lord could not ignore or suppress such protests, since the ordinary person also farmed the lord's land. In the end, the protests forced the lords to observe the Peace of God, by having them swear a holy oath that in their fights and skirmishes, they would not harm noncombatants. This was soon followed by a further refinement, the Truce of God, which made belligerents take a holy oath that they would not fight on Sundays or on feast days.[15] These movements were popular in origin and were adopted by the Church, because the Church at this time was ineffectual and structurally weak.

The Vikings had focused their attacks on churches and monasteries, and this had made the position of individual holy places very precarious. And when rebuilding was begun after a destructive raid, the funds and resources were provided by the local lord. And once this lord gave money to build a church or a monastery or a convent, he assumed that the new building belonged to him and he could therefore control its revenue. To do so effectively, he took it upon himself to appoint the clergy; these appointees were often members of the lord's own family, who had little or no training in matters theological or liturgical. Also, such appointees ended up selling their holy office to the highest bidder (a church's revenue depended on land as well as offerings, which made the job of a priest attractive). This was the practice of simony, which by the eleventh century had thoroughly permeated the entire hierarchy of the Church, right up to the office of the pope itself.[16]

But again there was discontent among the ordinary people, since they could not be sure if a person who had no training or education to be a priest could actually perform the rites of the Church—and whether these rites had any legitimacy or spiritual benefit. This discontent spread also into certain members of the nobility. One such noble was Saint Gerald (855–909 AD), who established a new monastery at Aurillac, in the Auvergne region of France. But instead of putting a relative in charge of it and siphoning off its revenues, Gerald granted this new monastery complete independence from all secular or state influence. In fact, he placed the monastery directly under the protection of the pope, which was unheard of.[17] Such piety was shared by a far more powerful lord, Duke William I of Aquitaine (875–918 AD), who founded a new monastery at Cluny, in Burgundy, where he had a hunting lodge and some land he never used; and he too gave it complete independence.[18] This simple act of devotion further strengthened the reforming trend in the Church that would see it become an independent spiritual institution and not simply an extension of the state.[19] Soon, many other monasteries and churches began to demand similar freedom from their various secular lords.[20] This demand was strengthened by the adoption of the Peace and Truce of God movements by Cluny. And the power the Church had over the lords was twofold. First, it offered assurance and security in the life to come through prayers and masses. Second, it could channel divine grace for immediate benefits through saints' relics.[21] This assurance and grace was the spiritual currency of the Middle Ages; without it life was entirely without meaning.

This reform slowly worked its way upward, for the popes themselves owed their office to the nobility. But curiously, papal reforms and the subsequent rise of the papacy were the result of simony. In 1044, Pope Benedict IX sold his office twice: first to Silvester III, who died quickly and Benedict again became pope; second to Gregory VI, who, despite his own simony, fervently wanted to reform the Church. Benedict was not pleased with what Gregory wanted to do and declared him a simoniac and himself the true pope. This led to much unrest and chaos among the people, both lay and cleric. To settle things, the powerful Henry III, the Holy Roman Emperor, marched into Rome, got rid of both Benedict and Gregory, and chose another man to become pope (Clement II). But in less than a year, Clement was dead. The Emperor installed another pope, Damasus II, but he died just twenty-three days into his papacy. Finally, Henry made his own cousin pope, namely Leo IX, who happened to be very reform minded. Leo set in motion the process that would make the Church entirely independent of the state. He eradicated the practice of simony. He enforced clerical celibacy. And he ensured that priests were properly educated in theology and Church doctrine. Most important of all, he established the College of Cardinals as a body that would study issues and concerns important to the faith. This allowed the Church to centralize its authority by breaking away from secular control and placing itself under the control of God Himself.[22]

The reforms became more radical under the next pope, Nicholas II. First, the Council of Cardinals prohibited lay investiture, or the choosing and installation of the clergy by the local lord. Second, in 1059, the Papal Election Decree was issued, which established that henceforth the only way a man could become pope was by being elected to the office by the Council of Cardinals. Secular lords could no longer put a pope in office. The Church had become free of state control. This decision did not sit well with many rulers, and Gregory was openly and violently opposed by Henry IV, the king of the Germans and the new Holy Roman Emperor, who wanted to regain the lost privileges of the state. This led to the great Investiture Controversy, which plunged Europe once again into bloody conflict and chaos.[23] However, the popes now had powerful supporters in the Normans of southern Italy, who had carved up a principality for themselves right up to Capua and Benevento, taking away lands from both the Lombard rulers and the Byzantines.[24] They belonged to highly successful families of adventurers from Normandy, such as the Drengots and the Hautevilles. Members of the Hauteville clan had fought many battles against Byzantium, men such as Robert

Guiscard (1015–1085) and his son Bohemond (1058–1111), both of whom consolidated the Norman hold on southern Italy and parts of present-day Macedonia and Greece.[25]

Further, the economic basis of Europe had changed—cities replaced villages as places of commercial activity. This change strengthened the Church as well, by increasing the role and function of the bishop—for a city was also a diocese in which the bishop functioned as the spiritual head. In the earlier rural economies of village life, that role was fulfilled by the abbot of a monastery. Thus, the papacy consolidated its authority by making bishops answerable to the pope, who represented Christ. In this way, the hierarchy of the Church acquired its authority not from the state but from God. Thus, by the time Urban II became pope in 1088, the Church was a tightly organized institution, self-sustaining and independent, that could marshal, direct, and control a unified response from its faithful.

Like Western Europe, the Middle East had undergone a destabilization and then consolidation process. By the eleventh century the nomadic Turks were on the move from Central Asia.[26] One tribe, the Seljuqs, from the Kazakh Steppe, probed into Iran and gained supremacy in the province of Khorasan. And from there they slowly began to take over the Middle East up to, but not including, Egypt. In 1055 they took Baghdad, rendering the caliphate there, once the spiritual and political backbone of Islam, as ineffectual and peripheral. It was also at this time that they converted to the Sunni sect of Islam. Then they turned westward, and by about 1060 began to filter into Anatolia, which belonged both to Byzantium and Armenia. Matters came to a head in 1071 when the Byzantine army met the Seljuq Turks in battle at Manzikert.[27] The outcome was a disaster for the Byzantines; not only were they thoroughly defeated, but their emperor, Romanus IV Diogenes, was captured. It did not take the Turks long to consolidate their hold on Anatolia under the able leadership of Alp Arslan (1029–1072), including the capture of Armenia. They established the Seljuq Sultanate of Rum, which would become the foundation of what is now Turkey.[28] For the Christians in these areas, there was severer oppression. The pope at the time, Gregory VII, called for an army to be raised to fight the Muslims and defend the eastern Christians. He may well have succeeded in launching such a campaign had he not become embroiled in the Investiture Controversy, which destabilized his papacy and much of Europe.

However, a strong emperor had come to the throne in Constantinople, namely Alexius I Comnenus (1048–1118), who effected important economic and social reforms that saw prestige and influence return to Byzantium, and he sought to normalize relationships with the papacy and the West.[29] He restructured the military so that it might effectively contend with the Turks, raising more mercenaries from England (largely disaffected Anglo-Saxons who had fled after the Norman invasion of 1066 led by William the Conqueror) as well as Bulgars, Pechenegs, and even Turks.[30] However, Alexius still had much trouble with the Seljuqs. He wanted to retake Anatolia. But to do so, he would need more soldiers than he presently had. He turned to the West and sent his ambassadors to the new pope, namely Urban II, who was friendly to Byzantium.[31]

The ambassadors arrived at Piacenza, where a church council was to meet from March 1 to 5, 1095, and there they asked for help in driving the Seljuq Turks out of Anatolia. To emphasize the urgency of this request, they also reminded the pope and the council that pilgrimages to Jerusalem had become impossible for Christians, now that the Holy Land was in the possession of these same Turks. And there might also have been a hint of the unification of the Eastern and Western Churches after the Great Schism.[32] The appeal resonated strongly, and a few months later, at the Council of Clermont, Urban delivered his call for action, which would become the First Crusade.[33] The *Gesta* gives a summary of what the pope said as well as the great fervor this evoked among the people. And here it is important to note that the First Crusade was largely a Norman and French undertaking—and an undertaking by individual nobles. None of the European kings supported the pope—Philip I of France was an excommunicate, Henry IV of Germany was Urban's greatest foe, and Spain was engaged in fighting Muslims on its own soil. It would largely become a Norman expedition, with support from three members of the French nobility: Hugh I, Count of Vermandois (1053–1101); Raymond IV, Count of Toulouse (1041–1105); and Godfrey of Bouillon (1060–1100).

The call went out throughout France and Germany and was further spread by the fervid preaching of Peter the Hermit.[34] However, Urban had stipulated that only those who could afford to do so should go on the crusade, while women, children, and the enfeebled were to stay behind.[35] He also discouraged priests and monks from joining, stating that they served far more effectively through prayer. In time, some 150,000 people gathered to become pilgrims, ready to march off to the Holy Land. They were poor, they were both men and women, and they had no notion of what this pilgrimage entailed; some were even the unfit and ill, who no doubt wanted to go to the Holy Land in the hope of getting well. Of these, only about 20,000 made it all the way to the Near East. They were all killed, except those that converted. Thereafter the crusade fell into the far abler hands of the Normans and their allies.

But why would anyone want to become a crusader? To answer this question properly, it is important to understand the medieval mind-set. The Middle Ages were deeply rooted in Christianity, and this meant that God was central to all aspects of life, and He could be accessed through the structure of religion, that is, the Church.[36] No human endeavor existed outside a universal moral structure: good or evil—the choice was part of free will. It is in this context that the crusades are best examined, as pious acts. History, therefore, was pious history; it was history with a moral core that sought to guide humankind into attitudes and behavior contained within the framework of universal goodness, whereby the individual could become aligned to, and find a place in, God's grand program of redemption. This is the mind-set of all the individuals that went on the First Crusade, because for them it was not a matter of winning land, but winning salvation by seeking to do what they thought was pious. It was a pilgrimage taken to restore the connection between the individual and God. Since participation in the crusade was entirely voluntary, a crusader's final allegiance thus lay with God alone.

NATURE OF THE FIRST CRUSADE

As previously mentioned, the First Crusade occurred in two phases. The first, the People's Crusade, consisted of nothing more than an enthused rabble that believed it was simply enough to show up in the Near East and God would take care of the rest. Thus it had no military leadership other than that provided by Walter Sans-Avoir (wrongly called the Penniless, for he was far from poor), and it had no clear strategy other than allowing God to use the pilgrims as His instruments. The Turks, therefore, easily overcame them and slaughtered them, enslaving those who converted. In the second phase, known as the Princes' Crusade, the nobility led their own armies made up of professional warriors, who were accustomed to military tactics and maneuvers. Thus, it was the participants in the second phase, about 40,000 strong, who won the crusade and brought about the capture of the Levant and Jerusalem.

Also, three specific incidents in the course of the crusade are often commented upon and deserve closer scrutiny

Firstly, when Peter the Hermit preached the crusade in Cologne and the Rhineland, it spawned another sort of reaction—one that sought to exact vengeance from non-Christians closer at hand, namely the Jews.[37] This contingent of the People's Crusade was led by the lord of Leiningen, Count Emicho, who brought his followers down the Rhineland, from Speyer to Cologne, attacking Jews and taking their property. Of course, it also must be remembered that even to the medieval mind this was an aberration of the crusade ideal, and the Church actively sought to protect Jews. These attacks, though vicious, were not typical and were strongly condemned by the clergy of the day. But it is always difficult to insist on ideals, since mobs are motivated by various forces, just as it is equally wrong to use these various incidents to label all crusaders as regularly participating in anti-Jewish violence. Indeed, the violence against Jews happened mostly in Germany, where the Jews were quickly equated with the faraway Muslims. But this violent mob never got to the Near East: Count Emicho's followers were slaughtered by King Coloman of Hungary, and Emicho himself barely escaped with his life. Thereafter, the violence against the Jews dissipated. In other words, persecution of the Jews was not the focus of the First Crusade, which is why it was persistently decried and denounced by the Church. And it is important to note that the *Gesta* does not mention any violence against the Jews.

Secondly, there is the infamous incident of cannibalism at the siege of Marra. It is recorded in most of the chronicles of the First Crusade. The *Gesta* does mention it briefly, and recently a lot of scholarly ink has been spilled in trying to explain what exactly happened and why. These explanations range from describing this cannibalism as a sacral act[38] or as the manifestation of Western cultural superiority, as a literal devouring of the alien Other,[39] or even as a form of Holy Communion, since the crusaders saw themselves as the materialization of God's justice on earth.[40] In the final analysis perhaps this is all an overintellectualization of war's brutality by scholars who wish to seek some rational, philosophical, or psychological understanding of what happened. Despite its ideal nature, the First Crusade was also a war; like all wars it was nasty, brutish, and cruel, and this was evident both on the Turkish side and on the side of the crusaders. Thus, this incident of cannibalism suggests only two possibilities. First, the few crusaders that practiced it were simply insane with hunger—throughout the *Gesta* mention is made again and again of the unending struggle to just find something to eat and to have some water to drink—and the sheer agony when there is nothing. In one extreme case of suffering from thirst, the crusaders soak rags in cesspits (open latrines) in order to have any kind of liquid to drink, or they resort to drinking their own urine. This certainly indicates intense suffering. The occurrence of cannibalism is also the result of such unrelenting physical suffering through hunger. And second, if a detailed analysis really is necessary, this incident must be read in the context in which it occurs (a context often missed by commentators on this incident): The cannibalism happens immediately after the crusaders begin cutting open the guts of the Turkish dead to retrieve bezants and small precious items. This, of course, means that many of the Turkish inhabitants of Marra had swallowed their valuables to transport them safely away from the crusaders. Many of these never made it to safety. The cutting open of the bodies to extract these precious objects and the resultant cannibalism (practiced not by all, but a few) are to be read together; the one leads to another. When the Turkish dead are cut open to extract what valuables they might have swallowed while alive, their bodies become simply flesh; and it is not a great leap for the soldiers involved in such acts to think of roasting the flesh and eating it because they are hungry—for the crusaders are perpetually near starvation. War and severe privation dehumanize people. This is the only thing to be understood from the incident of cannibalism at Marra. To read it as indicative of cultural or philosophical positions of the crusaders is simply a failure to come to grips with the necessary and wretched brutality of war.

Thirdly, there is the slaughter by the crusaders of the inhabitants of Jerusalem. The *Gesta* relates that the streets ran ankle-deep in blood.

Like so many such details in medieval chronicles, this is a trope of the utter destruction of the enemy. It should not be taken literally. It is true that a lot of the inhabitants of Jerusalem were killed by the crusaders, but it is also true that many were not. Thus, a medieval trope needs to be "stylistically" read—the enemy that had defiled the holy city of Jerusalem has been entirely destroyed. To the medieval mind, this meant that the good had vanquished evil—the ideal war is always a total war.[41]

In effect, the destruction of Jerusalem described in the *Gesta* is "biblical" in proportion and style and must be read as such. Here, for example, is a passage from the Bible that describes such destruction: "Then Joshua turned back at that time, and captured Hazor and struck its king with the sword; for Hazor formerly was the head of all these kingdoms. They struck every person who was in it with the edge of the sword, utterly destroying them; there was no one left who breathed. And he burned Hazor with fire. Joshua captured all the cities of these kings, and all their kings, and he struck them with the edge of the sword, and utterly destroyed them; just as Moses the servant of the Lord had commanded. However, Israel did not burn any cities that stood on their mounds, except Hazor alone, which Joshua burned. All the spoil of these cities and the cattle, the sons of Israel took as their plunder; but they struck every man with the edge of the sword, until they had destroyed them. They left no one who breathed. Just as the Lord had commanded Moses his servant, so Moses commanded Joshua, and so Joshua did; he left nothing undone of all that the Lord had commanded Moses. Thus Joshua took all that land: the hill country and all the Negev, all that land of Goshen, the lowland, the Arabah, the hill country of Israel and its lowland from Mount Halak, that rises toward Seir, even as far as Baalgad in the valley of Lebanon at the foot of Mount Hermon. And he captured all their kings and struck them down and put them to death. Joshua waged war a long time with all these kings. There was not a city which made peace with the sons of Israel except the Hivites living in Gibeon; they took them all in battle. For it was of the Lord to harden their hearts, to meet Israel in battle in order that he might utterly destroy them, that they might receive no mercy, but that he might destroy them, just as the Lord had commanded Moses" (Joshua 11: 10–20). It is in such a biblical landscape, setting, and context that the crusaders themselves moved.

TRANSLATION

This translation is based upon the published editions of the *Gesta* that have been edited by Bongars, Le Bas, Hagenmeyer, Bréhier, and Hill,[42] as well as personal consultation of the manuscript tradition. It includes the complete *Gesta* as it has been preserved, as well as the description of the holy places in Jerusalem, the prayers for the Mass of the Holy Sepulcher, and for the first time, the quatrain in praise of Bohemond, and the list of four names that concludes the *Gesta* portion of the Vatican manuscript *Reginensis latini 641*.

The place names in the *Gesta* have been left unchanged as they appear in the original Latin, although some personal names have been translated since they are well known in the field of crusade studies. Also, the archaisms prevalent in the previous two English translations have been avoided, especially in the case of Hill, who takes excessive and needless liberties with the original.[43] The rough and simple Latin of the *Gesta* and the many repetitious phrases are clearly stylistic choices made by the original authors; and so it is the intent of this translation to not allow editorial outlook to skewer or color what the *Gesta* has to say. It is the earliest account of the First Crusade, and that is indeed wonder enough.

THE DEEDS OF THE FRANKS
AND OTHER JERUSALEMITES

The First Narrative

Year-End 1095 to February 1097

POPE URBAN II PREACHES
THE FIRST CRUSADE—NOVEMBER 1095

*W*hen that time came, foretold to his faithful by the Lord Jesus, especially in the Gospel, in which he says: "If anyone would come after me, he must deny himself and take up his cross and follow me,"[1] there was a great awakening in all the regions of Gaul,[2] so that anyone, with a pure heart and spirit, who diligently sought to follow the Lord and would carry the cross after Him, did not tarry but in all haste sought out the road to the Holy Sepulcher.

Indeed, the Apostle of the See of Rome,[3] Urban the Second,[4] hastened to the lands beyond the mountains[5] with his archbishops, bishops, abbots, and priests and began to speak and deliver shrewd sermons, saying that if anyone would save his soul, let him humbly take the path of the Lord, and if he lacked the deniers,[6] divine mercy would provide. And then the lord Apostle also added: "Brothers, much must you suffer for the name of Christ—even destitution, poverty, nakedness, persecutions, adversity, sickness, hunger, thirst, and other such evils—as the Lord said to his disciples: 'Greatly must you suffer for my name.'[7] And: 'Be not ashamed to speak in front of men; I shall give you the voice and the eloquence.'[8] And again: 'Great shall be your reward.'"[9]

DEPARTURE OF THE CRUSADERS—APRIL 1096

Now as these words spread little by little through all the fatherland of Gaul, the Franks, hearing these words, began to sew the cross, without delay, on their right shoulders, declaring that they would, to a man, follow in the footsteps of Christ by whom they had been ransomed from the power of Tartarus.[10]

And then the Gauls at once forsook their homes, and these same Gauls formed themselves into three parts.[11] One part of the Franks went into the region of Hungary, that is, with Peter the Hermit[12] and Duke Godfrey[13] and Baldwin his brother[14] and Baldwin, count of Mons.[15] These most powerful warriors[16] and many others, whom I do not know,[17] went by the road which Charlemagne, the wondrous king of Francia,[18] once had constructed all the way to Constantinople.[19]

PETER THE HERMIT AT CONSTANTINOPLE—JULY 30, 1096

The above-mentioned Peter was the first to reach Constantinople on the third calends of August,[20] and with him were very many German people.[21] There he found gathered the Longobards[22] and many others. The emperor[23] had ordered that they be given supplies as were readily available in the city, and he said to them: "Do not cross over the Arm[24] before the bulk of the Christians arrive, because you are not numerous enough to fight the Turks." However, these very same Christians gave themselves over to wickedness, for they destroyed and burned the palaces of the city, and they removed the lead with which the roofs of the churches were covered and sold it to the Greeks. For this reason the emperor was angry and gave the order for them to cross over the Arm.

THE PEOPLE'S CRUSADE

After they had crossed over, they did not cease from doing all kinds of evil deeds, burning and devastating homes and churches.[25] Finally they reached Nicomedia[26] where the Longobards and the Germans separated from the Franks, because the Franks were bloated with pride. The Longobards chose a man to rule over them named Rainald.[27] The Germans did likewise, and then all of them went into Romania.[28] And they marched for four days beyond the city of Nicaea[29] and came upon a castle named Exerogorgo,[30] which was empty of all people; and they took it and found inside enough grain and wine and meat and all other good things in abundance.

THE TURKISH ATTACK—SEPTEMBER 29, 1096

However, when the Turks heard that the Christians were in the castle, they came and besieged it. Now, in front of the gates of the castle was a well and at the foot of the castle was a living spring near which Rainald came and laid an ambush for the Turks. But when the Turks arrived on the day dedicated to Saint Michael,[31] they discovered Rainald and those that were with him and the Turks slaughtered many of them. The rest fled into the castle. The Turks laid siege to the castle and deprived those inside of water. So terribly did our men suffer from thirst that they cut open the veins of their horses and donkeys and drank the blood; others lowered their belts and rags down into the cesspits and squeezed the liquid into their mouths; and others urinated into the cupped hands of companions and drank it up; and still others dug into the damp earth and lying upon their backs piled up the earth upon their chests, so parched were they from thirst. Indeed the bishops and presbyters comforted our men and exhorted them to hold fast.

This tribulation lasted for eight days. Then Rainald, leader of the Germans, made a pact with the Turks that he would betray his companions, and feigning to go forth and fight he fled to the Turks and many went with him. All those who refused to renounce the Lord were given the capital sentence.[32] Others that were captured alive were divided up like sheep. Still others were used as targets for arrows. And the remainder they sold or gave away like animals. Then they took their prizes home, some to Khorasan,[33] some to Antioch,[34] and some to Aleppo,[35] or wherever they lived.

Such were the first ones to accept martyrdom in the name of the Lord Jesus.

MASSACRE AT CIVETOT—OCTOBER 21, 1096

Then the Turks heard that Peter the Hermit and Walter Sans-Avoir[36] were to be found in Civetot,[37] which is just above the city of Nicaea, and they came there with great joy that they might kill them and those that were with them. When the Turks got there, they came upon Walter with his men and quickly killed them. However, Peter the Hermit, not long before, had returned to Constantinople, since he could not control such a diverse mass of men who did not want to obey him or heed his words.[38] The Turks fell upon them and killed a great number. Some they found asleep, others naked—and all these they put to death. Among them was a priest who was celebrating Mass whom they made a martyr, right on the altar.[39] Those who were able to get away fled to Civetot, and some hurled themselves into the sea; others hid themselves in the woods and mountains. And some the Turks chased into the castle, and they heaped up wood to burn them and the castle.[40]

Now the Christians that were inside the castle set fire to the piles of wood, and the flame turned against the Turks and burned a certain number of them. But God preserved our men from being burned in that fire. After some time, the Turks captured them alive and divided them all among themselves, as they had done earlier with the others, and then they dispersed them through all the regions, some to Khorasan, others to Persia.[41] All this happened in the month of October.[42]

When the emperor heard that the Turks had dispersed our men in this way, great was his joy and he gave the order that those who survived could again cross the Arm. And when they came over, he took away all their weapons.[43]

ARRIVAL OF THE OTHER
CRUSADERS—OCTOBER TO NOVEMBER 1096

The second part[44] entered Sclavonia,[45] along with Raimond, count of Saint Gilles,[46] and the bishop of Puy.[47]

The third part went by the old Roman road.[48] Among them were Bohemond,[49] Richard the Principate,[50] Robert count of Flanders,[51] Robert the Norman,[52] Hugh Magnus,[53] Evrard of Puiset,[54] Achard of

Montmerle,[55] Isoard of Mouzon,[56] and many others. And they came to the ports, some at Brindisi, some at Bari, and some at Otranto.[57]

Then Hugh Magnus and William the son of the Marquis[58] took to the sea from the port of Bari and landed at Durres. Now the duke of that place,[59] when he heard that such valiant and trustworthy men were landing, conceived of an evil plan in his heart. He apprehended them and cautiously sent them to Constantinople that they might swear an oath of fidelity before the emperor.

DUKE GODFREY'S ARRIVAL—DECEMBER 23, 1096

And at the very last, Duke Godfrey, the first among all the leaders, arrived at Constantinople with a great army; he came two days before the Nativity of our Lord and set up camp outside the city, until that sinful emperor commanded that he be given lodging in the faubourg of the city.

Having moved into his living quarters, the Duke, without much concern for security, sent out his warriors each day to gather straw and other things needed by the horses. Now they believed that they could go wherever they wanted to in complete confidence. But the sinful emperor Alexius commanded the Turcopoles[60] and Pechenegs[61] to attack them and kill them.

ATTACK ON THE CRUSADERS BY THE IMPERIAL ARMY—JANUARY 13, 1097

Now when Baldwin, the duke's brother, heard about this, he set up an ambush, and he surprised them while they were killing his own people, and with a valiant spirit he attacked them and, with God's help, overcame them. He captured sixty of them, killing some and giving the rest to his brother the duke.

But when the emperor heard of this, he was extremely angry. Seeing that the emperor was furious, the duke left the city with his men and set up camp outside the city. As the evening came on, the devious emperor ordered his men to attack the duke and the Christian people. But the invincible duke, leading the soldiers of Christ, routed them; he himself killed seven and chased the others right up to the gates of the city. Then he returned to his camp where he remained for five days until he concluded a pact with the emperor, and the emperor told him to cross over the Arm of Saint George, and that he would allow him to restock his supplies as much as Constantinople could permit; as well that he would give alms so that the poor might be able to live and sustain themselves.[62]

BOHEMOND TAKES THE CROSS—JUNE OR JULY 1096

Now, Bohemond, the mighty in war, who was besieging Amalfi at the Bridge of Scafati,[63] heard that innumerable Christian people, mostly Franks, had arrived and were determined to proceed to the Sepulcher of our Lord[64] and were prepared to fight against pagan people. He then diligently inquired as to what type of weapons they fought with, what emblem of Christ they carried as they went their way, and what war cry they shouted in battle. This was the response he received, and in this order: "They are properly armed for battle; either on the right shoulder or between the shoulders they wear the cross of Christ; and their war cry is: 'God wills it! God wills it! God wills it!' which they all shout in one voice." And, inspired by the Holy Spirit, Bohemond at once ordered that the most costly cloak he possessed be cut up and the pieces made into crosses.

And then the vast majority of the warriors that were besieging the city with him dashed to him, so ardent was their desire—so much so that Count Roger was left nearly all by himself, and he returned to Sicily, mourning and lamenting the loss of all his men.

BOHEMOND SETS OUT FOR
THE CRUSADE—CA. OCTOBER 26, 1096

Lord Bohemond, when he returned to his own land, prepared with great zeal to take the path to the Holy Sepulcher, until he crossed over the sea with his army.[65] And with him were Tancred, son of the Marquis,[66] and Prince Richard[67] and Rainulf his brother,[68] and Robert of Anse,[69] Herman of Canny,[70] Robert of Sourdeval,[71] Robert son of Tostain,[72]

Humphrey son of Radulf,[73] Richard son of Count Rainulf,[74] the count of Russinolo along with his brothers,[75] Boel of Chartres,[76] Albered of Cagnano,[77] and Humphrey of Monte Scabioso.[78] All of these crossed over in the service of Bohemond and landed at Bulgaria where they found an abundance of grain and wine and all kinds of food for the body.

Afterward, they went down into the valley of Andronopolis,[79] and there they waited for all their people to make their way down. Then Bohemond held a council with his men to give them courage and to exhort them to be good and to be humble and not to ravage this land which belonged to Christians and to take only that which they needed to nourish themselves.

BOHEMOND ARRIVES AT CASTORIA—CHRISTMAS DAY 1096

Then setting out and passing through great richness and prosperity from farmland to farmland, from city to city, from castle to castle, we[80] arrived at Castoria,[81] where we solemnly celebrated the Nativity of our Lord. And we stayed there several days and looked to purchasing supplies. But the people would not agree to sell us any because they were very frightened of us, for they refused to see us as pilgrims but as men come to devastate their land and to kill them. Therefore we stole cattle, horses, and donkeys and whatever else we could find.[82]

Upon leaving Castoria, we entered Palagonia,[83] where a town of heretics was located.[84] We attacked it from all sides and very soon it came under our control, and lighting a fire we burned the town along with its inhabitants.[85]

THE BATTLE OF VARDAR—FEBRUARY 18, 1097

After this, we came to the river Vardar,[86] and lord Bohemond crossed over along with his men, but not all of them, because the count of Russignolo remained behind with his brothers. Then the army of the emperor came and attacked the count and his brothers and all who were with them.

Now when Tancred heard of this, he went back and threw himself into the river and swam across to the others; and two thousand men also threw themselves into the river and followed Tancred. They found Turcopoles and Pechenegs fighting against our men and they made a quick, vigorous, and strategic attack and were victorious. They captured many and then led them, all bound, in front of the lord Bohemond, who said to them: "Why, wretches, did you slaughter Christ's men and mine? I have no quarrel with your emperor." And they responded: "We could not do otherwise, for we are in the pay of the emperor and whatever he commands, we must do." And Bohemond let them go unpunished.[87]

This battle was fought on the fourth day of the week which was the beginning of Lent.[88] Blessed be God in all things. Amen.

Here ends the first book. Here begins the second book.

The Second Narrative

February 20 to June 19, 1097

BOHEMOND IS ESCORTED INTO
CONSTANTINOPLE—FEBRUARY 20, 1097

The miserable emperor, at the same time that we sent our messengers, commanded at last one of his men who was very close to him, and whom they call the curopalate,[1] to guide us safely through his land until we arrived at Constantinople. So whenever we passed by their cities, he commanded the inhabitants of that land to bring us supplies, as was done by those of whom we have already spoken. Indeed, so fearful were they of the men of lord Bohemond that they permitted none of our men to get past the walls of their cities.

Now, our men wanted to attack and capture one such town because it was filled with all kinds of supplies. But Bohemond, a wise man, would not consent to it, for it was exempted land[2] and also because he had given his promise to the emperor. And for this reason was he angry with Tancred and with all the others. This happened in the evening. And in the morning, the inhabitants came out of the town in a procession, holding crosses, and went before Bohemond. Gladly he received them and sent them away rejoicing.

ARRIVAL AT SERRES AND RUSA—END OF FEBRUARY 1097

Afterward, we came to a certain city called Serres,[3] where we set up our tents and where we had good provisions for that time of year.[4] And it was there that Bohemond met with two curopalates, and out of friendship for them and because it was exempted land, he commanded that all the animals that our men had stolen be returned.

After that we came to the city of Rusa.[5] The Greek people came out and joyously met lord Bohemond and brought us a lot of supplies; and there we set up our pavilions on the Wednesday before our Lord's Last Supper. And then Bohemond left all his men behind and made his way to Constantinople to confer with the emperor; he took with him only a few warriors.

Tancred stayed behind as the head of the army of Christ, and seeing the pilgrims buying cooked food, he decided to abandon the main road and to lead the men to a place where they could stay more comfortably. And he led them into a valley which was filled with all good things that nourish the body, and there with great devotion we celebrated our Lord's feast day of Easter.[6]

BOHEMOND ARRIVES AT CONSTANTINOPLE—APRIL 10, 1097

When the emperor heard that a most honorable man, Bohemond, had come to see him, he commanded that he be received with honor, but with due caution he had him lodged outside the city. When he had been lodged, the emperor asked him to come and confer with him in secret. Duke Godfrey and his brother also took part, and the count of Saint-Gilles was not far from the city.

OATHS OF ALLEGIANCE TO THE EMPEROR—APRIL 1097

Now the emperor, anxious and boiling with rage, wanted to find some way, either by ruse or by fraud, to capture these soldiers of Christ. But by divine grace, neither he nor his men could find the place or opportunity to bring them harm. Instead, all the highborn men that were to be found in Constantinople gathered together, and out of fear for the loss of their land, they took counsel and drew up ingenious schemes that our dukes, counts, and all other leaders should swear an oath of loyalty to the emperor. But they all refused, saying, "Indeed, this is not worthy of us, and it does not seem fair to us that we should be swearing any sort of oath to him."[7]

But perhaps once more we were deceived by our leaders, for what did they do in the end? They said that necessity forced them willingly or unwillingly, to humble themselves before the will of the emperor.[8]

Now the emperor greatly feared Bohemond, that bravest of men, who had chased him and his army from the battlefield more than once,[9] and he said to him that if he freely swore loyalty to him, he would give him land beyond Antioch, the breadth of which would take fifteen days to cover and the width of which would take eight days to cover. And he swore that he would remain true to his word, if Bohemond remained true to his oath.

Why did such brave and strong warriors do such a thing? Without a doubt because they were driven by the direst need.[10]

And so the emperor gave all our men assurance and promised them security; and he even promised that he would accompany us with his army by land and by sea, and that he would faithfully ensure that we got our supplies by land and by sea, and to diligently restore all our losses, and further that he would neither want nor permit anyone to harm or trouble our pilgrims on the road to the Holy Sepulcher.

THE COUNT OF SAINT-GILLES AND TANCRED REFUSE TO SWEAR AN OATH—APRIL 1097

Now, the count of Saint-Gilles was staying outside the city in the faubourg, and his men had remained behind. And the emperor commanded the count to come and do homage and swear loyalty to him, as the others had done. But as the emperor was sending this message, the count was planning on how he might get revenge from the imperial army. However, Duke Godfrey and Robert, count of Flanders, and the other princes said to him that it was not right to fight against Christians. And then that wise man, Bohemond, said that if the count did the emperor any injustice, or did not swear allegiance to him, he himself would take the part of the emperor. Thereupon the count, having taken counsel of his men, swore to respect the life and honor of Alexius, and would never consent to harm the emperor, either by his own deed or by the deed of one of his men. When he was called to swear allegiance, he responded that he would do nothing of the sort, even if his head was at stake.[11] And so the men of lord Bohemond approached Constantinople.

Now, Tancred and Richard the Principate crossed over the Arm stealthily, because they did not want to swear allegiance to the emperor; and with them went almost all of Bohemond's men. And soon the army of the count of Saint-Gilles came up to Constantinople, and the count remained there with his men. Bohemond also remained with the emperor so that he could take counsel with him on how to supply the men who had already gone beyond Nicaea. It was Duke Godfrey who was the first to go to Nicomedia, along with Tancred and all the rest. And they stayed there for three days.

THE CRUSADERS CAMP AT NICAEA—MAY 6, 1097

But the duke saw that there existed no good road by which he might lead his men to the city of Nicaea, because the road that was there,[12] and which had been used by earlier pilgrims,[13] was not wide enough to allow so many men to pass through. And so he sent ahead three thousand men, with axes and swords, and told them to go and cut and widen the road for our pilgrims, all the way up to the city of Nicaea. The road that they opened up led through the passes of a huge mountain,[14] and they left behind crosses made of iron and wood, placed upon stakes that they might serve as markers for our pilgrims. Finally we came up to Nicaea, which is the capital of all Romania. It was the fourth day of the Nones of May,[15] and there we set up our camp.

Before the arrival of lord Bohemond, there was such a dearth of bread among us that just one loaf sold for twenty or thirty deniers.[16] But after the wise Bohemond arrived, he brought a profusion of provisions by sea. And these poured in, from land and from sea, so that there was much abundance for the army of Christ.

THE SIEGE OF NICAEA—MAY 14, 1097

On the day of the Lord's Ascension,[17] we began to attack the city from all sides, and we built wooden siege engines[18] and wooden towers, by means of which we could knock down the towers on the walls. With much bravery and much strength we attacked the city for two days, and then we dug underneath the walls of the city.[19] The Turks who were inside the city sent a message to those that had come to the aid of the city,[20] telling them to come boldly and safely and to enter through the middle gate where no one was there to stand in their way and to attack them.[21]

But this gate on that very day, which was the Saturday after the Lord's Ascension, was taken by the count of Saint-Gilles and the bishop of Puy. This count came from the other side of the city; and protected by divine grace and resplendent in his earthly armor at the head of his army, encountered the Turks, who were advancing against our men. Shielded on all sides by the sign of the cross, he fell upon them fiercely and drove them back; they took to flight, leaving behind many dead. But the auxiliary Turks came to the aid of the rest, full of joy and exulting in certain victory, carrying with them ropes with which they would bind us and lead us off to Khorasan. They came rejoicing and slowly descended from the height of the mountain.[22] But all those who came down had their heads cut off by the hands of our men. And by means of a sling, our men hurled the heads of the dead into the city, in order to spread fear among the Turks.[23]

Then the count of Saint-Gilles and the bishop of Puy took counsel as to how they could dig underneath one of the towers which stood in front of their tents. They chose men who would dig underneath, along with arbalests and archers to protect them. They dug down to the foundations of the wall and piled beams and wood, and then they set fire to it all. It was evening when this was done, and the tower fell when it was night; because it was so dark there was no way we could fight them. During the night, the Turks got up hurriedly and restored the wall so solidly that when daylight came, there was no possibility of causing any damage from that side.

Before long, Robert count of Normandy and Count Stephen[24] and many others arrived; and then came Roger of Barneville.[25] Now

Bohemond besieged the city on the first front, and beside him was Tancred, and then Duke Godfrey and then the count of Flanders, and next to him was Robert of Normandy, and next to him the count of Saint-Gilles, and beside him was the bishop of Puy. Indeed, the land blockade was such that no one could leave the city nor enter it; and on this occasion all were come together as one.[26] Who could number such an army of Christ? No one, I believe, has ever seen or will ever see so many accomplished warriors.

But there was a huge lake on one side of the city upon which the Turks launched boats,[27] and thus they could leave and reenter with forage, wood, and much else besides. Then our leaders took counsel together and sent messengers to Constantinople to appeal to the emperor to have boats brought from Civetot, where there was a port, and to order that oxen be gathered to drag these boats over the mountains and through the forests and to the lake. This was done at once, and the emperor also sent his Turcopoles with them. On the day when the boats were brought in this fashion, they were not put into the water right away. But when night came, they were launched on the lake, full of well-armed Turcopoles. When it got light, the boats could be seen in the middle of the lake, moving against the city. The Turks marveled when they saw them, not knowing whether they were their own men or the emperor's. When they recognized them as the emperor's men, they were frightened to death, weeping and lamenting. And the Franks rejoiced and gave glory to God.

THE TURKS SURRENDER—JUNE 26, 1097

Then the Turks, seeing that no help would come to them from their army, sent a legation to the emperor, offering to give up the city if they might be allowed to leave with their wives, their children, and their goods. Then the emperor, full of vanity and iniquity, ordered that they could leave unpunished and without any fear and had them brought to Constantinople in great faithfulness. He dealt with them gently so that they might the more set up ambushes and obstacles for the Franks.

This siege lasted seven weeks and three days. Many of our men received martyrdom there, and with joy and elation gave their blissful souls to God. Among the poor, many died of hunger in the name of Christ.[28] Those who rose triumphant to heaven, put on the robe of martyrdom,[29] and proclaimed in one voice: "Avenge, O Lord, our blood which was shed for You, You who are blessed and worthy of praise from age to age. Amen."[30]

Here ends the second book. Here begins the third book.

The Third Narrative

The Crusaders in Asia Minor—July 1097

THE BATTLE OF DORYLAEUM—JULY 1, 1097

*M*eanwhile, the city fell, and the Turks were led off to Constantinople, where the emperor, who rejoiced more and more that the city had fallen into his power once again, commanded that alms be generously distributed among our poor. Now on the first day after our departure from the city,[1] we came to a certain bridge,[2] where we stayed for two days. On the third day, before the light of dawn, our men arose, and because it was so dark, they could not see to stay together on one path and became divided into two detachments, and traveled in this way for two days. In the first detachment were Bohemond, that brave man, and Robert of Normandy and the wise Tancred, and many others. In the second detachment were the count of Saint-Gilles and Duke Godfrey and the bishop of Puy and Hugh Magnus and the count of Flanders, and many others.

On the third day, the Turks ferociously attacked Bohemond and all those that were with him. Suddenly, these Turks began to let out shrieks and to jabber and shout in high-pitched voices, uttering I know not what diabolical sounds in their own tongue. That wise man, Bohemond, saw the numerous Turks far off in the distance letting off their shrieks and demonic clamor, and so he commanded all the warriors to dismount and to quickly pitch their tents. Before the tents were pitched, he again spoke to all the warriors: "High lords and bold warriors of Christ,

41

you can see how tough the fight is going to be, for we are surrounded. Therefore, let everyone fight manfully and let those who are on foot pitch the tents quickly and deftly."

By the time all this was done, the Turks had already encircled us and came at us from all sides, brandishing their weapons and hurling them, and shooting arrows from an incredible distance. And as for us, we knew we could not withstand them or hold the weight of so many enemies, but we went forward to meet them united as one. As for our women, they were a great help to us that day, bringing water to drink for the fighters, and no doubt even encouraging those who were fighting and defending. Then that wise man, Bohemond, at once sent a message to the others, that is, to the count of Saint-Gilles, to Duke Godfrey, to Hugh Magnus, to the bishop of Puy, and to all the other warriors of Christ, to tell them to hurry and come quickly to the battle, adding, "And if they want a fight today, they should come out manfully." And so Duke Godfrey, who was daring and brave, as well as Hugh Magnus, were the first ones to come along with their armies, and the bishop of Puy soon followed them with his own army, and then came the count of Saint-Gilles with a great many men.

Now, our men asked in astonishment from where had emerged such a multitude of Turks, Arabs, Saracens, and others whose names I do not know, because all the mountains, hills, and valleys, and all the flat places, inside and outside, were so completely filled with this race of excommunicates. Then a secret message was sent out among us, in which God was praised and counsel given, stating, "Come what may, stand firm in the faith of Christ and have faith in the victory of the Holy Cross, because today, if it pleases God, all riches shall be given you."

Our men fell into position on the battlefield. On the left side was that wise man, Bohemond, and Robert of Normandy and wise Tancred and Robert of Anse and Richard the Principate. The bishop of Puy advanced from another mountain in order to encircle the unbelieving Turks. Also on the left side rode that bravest of warriors, Raymond, and the count of Saint-Gilles. On the right side were Duke Godfrey and that most eager warrior, the count of Flanders, and Hugh Magnus, and many others whose names I do not know.

Now, as soon as our warriors came forward, the Turks, the Arabs, the Saracens, the Angulani,[3] and all the rest of the barbarous people at once ran away, over the mountains and out across the plains. Many were the Turks, Persians, Paulicians,[4] Saracens, Angulani, and other pagans who all numbered three hundred and sixty thousand, besides the Arabs whose number no man knows; only God knows. Indeed, they fled really quickly to their tents, but they did not linger very long there. They again took to flight, and we chased them and slaughtered them the whole day through. And we took much loot—gold, silver, horses, donkeys, camels, sheep, cattle, and so many other things that we did not know about. If the Lord had not been with us in battle, and if He had not quickly sent the other army into the field, none of us would have escaped, for we fought from the third hour to the ninth hour without stopping.[5] But God Almighty, merciful and kind, who did want His warriors to perish or fall into the hands of their enemies, sent us help quickly. But two of our honorable warriors were killed there, namely Godfrey of Monte Scabioso and William the son of the Marquis and brother of Tancred, and many others, as well as foot soldiers, whose names I do not know.

IN PRAISE OF TURKISH VALOR

Now, who can be wise and learned enough to dare to describe the wisdom, the martial qualities, and the courage of the Turks?[6] They thought that they could frighten Frankish men with the threat of their arrows, as they had terrified the Arabs, the Saracens, the Armenians, the Syrians, and the Greeks. But, may it please God, they shall never be as good as us. In truth, they say among themselves that they and the Franks are of one race, and that no other men are naturally born to be warriors as are the Franks and they. I will speak the truth, no one can argue against it—for if they had remained faithful to Christ and had held firmly to holy Christianity and had willingly confessed the one Lord in Trinity, and the one Son of God, born of a virgin, who suffered and who arose from the dead and who ascended into heaven in the sight of His disciples, and who sent the perfect consolation of the Holy Spirit—and if they had believed with right spirit and faith that He reigns in heaven and on earth, you would find no one who could match their strength, their courage, and their most ingenious ways of war. And so, by the grace of God, they were beaten by our men. This battle happened on the first day of July.

Here ends the third book. Here begins the fourth book.

The Fourth Narrative

The Crusaders March to Antioch—July to October 1097

THE DREADING OF SULEIMAN

The Turks, enemies of God and holy Christianity, after they were defeated, fled here and there, for four days and four nights. Now it happened that their leader, Suleiman, the son of Suleiman the Old,[1] who was fleeing from Nicaea, met ten thousand Arabs, who said to him: "O unfortunate man, more unfortunate than all our people, what terror are you fleeing from?"[2]

In tears Suleiman answered them: "Because once I had defeated all the Franks and had them bound to be led into captivity, and while I was having them tied up by turns, one to another, I looked behind me, and saw their men in such vast numbers that if you or anyone else had been there, it would have seemed to you that all the mountains, hills, valleys, and plains were covered by their multitude.[3] So when we saw them all, we suddenly and quickly took to the road, barely escaping from their hands. And this is why we are still so very frightened. And if you believe me and my words, run from here, because if they find out that even one of you is here, not one of you shall escape alive."

When they heard this tale, they turned back and vanished into all of Romania.

A DIRE MARCH THROUGH CENTRAL TURKEY—JULY AND AUGUST 1097

And we chased after these sinful Turks who fled from us each and every day. Whenever they came to a castle or a city, they deceived and fooled the inhabitants of that land,[4] saying, "We have defeated and overcome all the Christians, and not one of them will ever dare to rise up against us. Therefore let us enter in." And once they came in, they ransacked the churches and homes and other places and took away with them horses, donkeys, and mules, and gold and silver and anything else that they could carry. As well they took with them Christian children[5] and burned and destroyed everything that could be useful to us, even as they fled and trembled before our face. And so we pursued them through deserts and a land which was waterless and uninhabitable, from which we only just escaped and came out alive.[6] Hunger and thirst harassed us, and we had nothing to eat other than spiky plants which we plucked and crushed in our hands.[7] Such was the food on which we miserably survived. A great number of our horses died there, and as a result many of our mounted warriors became foot soldiers. For want of horses, our oxen became our riding animals, and because of such necessity our goats and sheep and dogs became our pack animals.

ARRIVAL AT ICONIUM—AUGUST 15, 1097

Eventually we came to enter a rich land, filled with delightful food for the body and all good things; and before long we arrived at Iconium.[8] The inhabitants[9] of this land warned and persuaded us to carry goatskins filled with water,[10] because only after a day's march there would be a great shortage of water. We did as they advised us, until we came to a river[11] where we encamped for two days.

SKIRMISH AT HERACLEA—AROUND SEPTEMBER 10, 1097

But our runners went on ahead until they came to Heraclea,[12] where a great number of Turks had gathered and lay in ambush, waiting to harm the warriors of Christ. The warriors of Almighty God boldly came upon these very Turks and attacked them valiantly. And that day our enemies were routed, fleeing quickly like an arrow, strongly shot, that flies from the bowstring. Then our men immediately entered the city, and thus we stayed there for four days.

TANCRED AND BALDWIN HEAD
FOR TARSUS, AROUND SEPTEMBER 14, 1097

At that time, Tancred, son of the Marquis and Count Baldwin, brother of Duke Godfrey, left the others and went into the valley of Botren-throt.[13] Tancred went his own way and came to Tarsus,[14] with his warriors. And the Turks emerged from that city as a large group and came forward to attack and fight the Christians. But our men advanced and fought and our men put the enemy to flight who fled as fast as possible back to the city. Indeed, Tancred, the warrior of Christ, slackened reins, rushed forward, and set up camp right in front of the city gate.

From the other side came Count Baldwin with his army, and he asked Tancred to amicably strike a bargain with him and consider sharing the city. But Tancred replied, "I refuse to make a pact with you in any way." When night came on, the Turks fled away, trembling, down to the last man. Then the inhabitants of the city came out in the dark of the night, calling out in loud voices: "Hurry up, invincible Franks, hurry up. For the Turks driven by fear of you have run off, fleeing in all directions."

TANCRED AND BALDWIN
QUARREL—AROUND SEPTEMBER 21, 1097

The new day arose, and the important men of the city came and freely surrendered the city and said to the two who were quarreling over it, "Let it be, good men of experience, let it be, for we ask and want that man to be our lord and prince who fought so manfully against the Turks yesterday." But Baldwin, that admirable count, bickered and quarreled, saying, "We should go into the city together and loot it, and he who can take the most can keep it, and he who can gather the most can gather it." To this the most valiant Tancred replied: "Far may such conduct be from me, for I do not want to plunder any Christians. The men of this city have chosen me to be lord over them, and it is me that they want." But Tancred, though he was a very brave man, could not argue against Count Baldwin, who had a very great army. And willing or not, he gave up the city and bravely drew back along with his army. And before long, two superb cities surrendered to him, namely, Athena and Manustra, as well as many castles.[15]

ARRIVAL AT CAESAREA—AROUND SEPTEMBER 27, 1097

Now, the main army, along with Raymond count of Saint-Gilles, the most learned Bohemond, and Duke Godfrey, and many others came into the land of the Armenians,[16] thirsting and eager for the blood of the Turks.

Thus they came to a certain castle which was so strong that nothing could prevail against it. With them, there was a man named Simeon,[17] who was born in that region, and he asked that he be given this land so that he might defend and keep it from the hands of the enemy, the Turks. The land was given to him, where he remained with his men. Then we left and happily came to Caesarea in Cappadocia.[18] Continuing on from Cappadocia, we came to a most beautiful and wealthy city[19] which, a little before we came to it, the Turks had been besieging for three weeks, but they could not conquer it. As soon as we arrived, it was placed into our hands with great joy. Then a certain warrior who was named Peter of Alpibus[20] asked all the lords to let him defend it in full faithfulness to God, to the Holy Sepulcher, to the lords, and to the emperor. And they freely granted him this, in great love.[21]

The following night, Bohemond heard that the Turks, who had been besieging the city, were not far in front of us. At once he and his warriors prepared to fight them wherever they might be, but they could not find them.

ARRIVAL AT COXON—OCTOBER 5–6, 1097

Thereafter, we came to a certain city named Coxon,[22] in which there was a great abundance of all goods that we were in need of. And thus the

Christians,[23] that is, those that lived in that city, at once surrendered to us, and we lived very well there for three days, and our men greatly recovered.

RECONNAISSANCE OF ANTIOCH AND THE ADVENTURES OF PETER OF ROASA—AROUND OCTOBER 7, 1097

Then, Count Raymond, hearing that the Turks who held Antioch had withdrawn, took counsel and decided to send some of his warriors that they might quickly occupy it. He chose those men who could do this, namely, the viscount Peter of Castellione,[24] William of Montpellier,[25] Peter of Roasa,[26] Peter Raymond of Pul,[27] along with five hundred warriors. And they came to a valley near Antioch, where stood a castle of the Paulicians, and there they heard that the Turks in the city were preparing to defend it strongly. Then Peter of Roasa separated from the rest, and the following night as he approached Antioch, he entered into the valley of Rugia,[28] where he found Turks and Saracens. He fought them and killed many of them and chased the rest into wild flight. And when the Armenians, who lived in that land, saw that he had so bravely defeated the pagans, they surrendered to him at once. Thus he took the city of Rusa[29] as well as many castles.

ARRIVAL AT ANTIOCH—OCTOBER 20, 1097

We others, who had remained behind, set out and began to cross over a diabolical mountain,[30] which was so high and precipitous that none of us dared go around another man on the track that lay along the side of the mountain. Horses fell off headlong, and one lead horse dragged down others with it. And the warriors stood wretchedly, wringing their hands in misery and agony, not knowing what to do with themselves and their arms. They wanted to sell their shields and splendid hauberks with helmets for no more than three or five deniers, or whatever they could get. Those who found no buyer simply threw them away and went on their way.

When we came through that execrable mountain, we came to a city called Marasim.[31] The inhabitants of that city came out and joyfully met our men and brought us a great supply of things. And we lived in abundance until lord Bohemond came. Thereafter, our warriors came into that valley in which the royal city of Antioch[32] is situated, which is the capital of all Syria, and which the Lord Jesus Christ gave to Peter the blessed, the prince of the Apostles, that it might be restored to the religion of the holy faith, through Him who abides and reigns with God the Father, in the unity of the Holy Spirit of God, from age to age. Amen.

Here ends the fourth book. Here begins the fifth book.

The Fifth Narrative

October to December 1097

APPROACH TO ANTIOCH—OCTOBER 20, 1097

*W*hen we approached the bridge of iron,[1] our forerunners, who went ahead of us, as was the custom, found in front of them innumerable Turks gathered together who were rushing to support Antioch. And so our men attacked them with one heart and with one resolve and overcame the Turks. The barbarians panicked and took to flight, and many of them were killed in that battle. Our men who had routed them, by the grace of God, took much loot—horses, camels, mules, donkeys laden with grain and wine.

THE SIEGE OF ANTIOCH—OCTOBER 21, 1097

Thereafter our men came and set up camp by the banks of a river,[2] and immediately that wise man Bohemond came to the front of the city gate, with four thousand warriors, and set up guard to make sure no one could leave or enter the city secretly at night. The next day, around midday, the rest of the army reached Antioch, on the fourth feast day which is the twelfth day before the calends of November.[3] And then we marvelously besieged three gates of the city. However, on the other side, we did not have enough space to set up a siege, because a mountain, high and shear, hindered us. In the meanwhile, the Turks, our enemy, who were inside the city, were so afraid of us that none of them dared attack us for a period of fifteen days. Soon we were living around the city, and we found a great abundance in the surroundings, namely much fruit on the vine, pits full of grain, trees with lots of apples on them, and many more good things that the body needs.

The Armenians and Syrians, who were inside the city, came out and showed themselves as if they were fleeing; daily they came to us, and all the while their wives were inside the city. They cleverly found out things from us, about our situation, and then reported everything back to those who were inside the city. After the Turks became sufficiently informed about everything that concerned us, they gradually began to come out of the city and began to hem us in, not only from one side, but wherever they could lie in ambush along our path, either toward the sea or toward the mountain.

EXPEDITION TO AREGH—NOVEMBER 18, 1097

Not far off lay a castle which was called Aregh[4] and where a great number of the bravest Turks had gathered, and who often harassed our men. Our leaders, when they heard of this, were very upset and troubled, and so they sent some of their warriors to diligently search for that place where the Turks were. When our men had found the place where they were hiding, our warriors, who were searching for them, went forth to meet them. But little by little our men fell back to where they knew Bohemond waited with his army. Very quickly two of our men were killed then. When Bohemond heard this he hurled forward with his men, like the boldest athlete of Christ.[5] The barbarians burst upon our men, for our men were few, who nevertheless joined battle. Indeed, many of our enemies were killed, and the captives were led before the city gate where they were beheaded in order to increase the suffering of those inside the city.

Some others came out of the city and got up on top of the gate and shot at us in such a way that their arrows fell into the enclosure of the camp of lord Bohemond; and one woman was killed by such an arrow.

A CASTLE IS BUILT—AROUND NOVEMBER 23, 1097

Consequently, all our leaders assembled and took counsel, saying, "Let us make a castle on top of Mount Maregart,[6] so that we may be safe and free of any fear of the Turks." And so the castle was constructed and fortified, and all the leaders took turns guarding it.

ANOTHER FOOD SHORTAGE—DECEMBER 1097

But, before Christmas, the grain we had taken and all foodstuffs that nourish the body began to run scarce. We no longer dared to venture out, and in the land of the Christians we could find nothing to eat. And no one dared to go into the land of the Saracens without a strong body of men. Finally, our chief lords took counsel as how best to rule so many men. And they decided in council that one part of our men should go and diligently try to gather provisions and protect the flanks of the army. And the other half should faithfully remain to protect the camp. Then Bohemond said, "High lords and most wise warriors, if you wish it and it seems good to you, I will be the one to go out with the count of Flanders."

EXPEDITION TO GET PROVISIONS—END
OF DECEMBER 1097

After we had gloriously and solemnly celebrated Christmas, they left on Monday, the second feast day,[7] and they took with them some twenty thousand warriors and foot soldiers and safely came into the land of the Saracens. Now there was a gathering of many Turks and Arabs and Saracens from Jerusalem and Damascus and Aleppo and from other regions as well who had come to help Antioch. They heard that Christian men had come into their country, and they began to prepare to battle the Christians. And at daybreak they came to that place where our people were gathered together. The barbarians split up into two companies, one in the front and one behind, so that they could encircle us from all sides. However, the illustrious count of Flanders, in all respects armed by faith and the sign of the cross, which he faithfully carried each and every day, charged out against them at the same time as Bohemond. With one aim, our men fell upon them, and they at once took to flight and quickly showed their backs, and left behind many dead. Our men took their horses and much other loot. Others who stayed alive quickly fled away and perished in that wrath prepared for destruction.[8] But our men returned in great joy, praising and magnifying the Three in One God who lives and reigns now and forever. Amen.

Here ends the fifth book. Here begins the sixth book.

The Sixth Narrative

The Siege of Antioch Continues—December 1097 to February 1098

SURPRISE ATTACK BY THE TURKS—DECEMBER 29, 1097

*T*hen the Turks, enemies of God and of holy Christianity, who were inside guarding the city of Antioch, heard that lord Bohemond and the count of Flanders were not among the besiegers, and so they came out of the city and boldly began to battle with our men, choosing to attack that part of the siege which was the weakest. Knowing well that the most valiant warriors were gone, they decided to come against us on a Tuesday and injure us.

Thus these dreadful barbarians came at night and vehemently fell upon us, killing many of our warriors and foot soldiers who were not cautious. On that bitter day, the bishop of Puy lost his seneschal who carried and protected his banner.[1] Had there not been a river between us,[2] they would have attacked us far more often and destroyed many more of our men.

LOOKING FOR PROVISIONS—JANUARY 1–2, 1098

And then that wise man, Bohemond, returned from the land of the Saracens and came to Tancred's mountain,[3] thinking that he might find something of value to carry away, for the entire land had been completely plundered. Some found something to carry away, others went away empty-handed. Then that wise man, Bohemond, reproached them, saying, "O, unhappy and miserable men! O, vilest of all Christians! Why do you want to return so quickly? Just wait, wait until we have gathered together as one, and do not run around like sheep that do not have a shepherd. If our enemies find you running about like this, they will slaughter you, because they have been watching day and night to find you separated from your leader, or all alone, and every day they work to either kill you or lead you into captivity." When he had finished speaking, he returned to his camp with his men, many of them empty-handed rather than laden with plunder.

When the Armenians and the Syrians saw that our men returned empty-handed, they got together and went up and down the mountains and into that country already mentioned and thoroughly searched for and bought grain and food for the body and brought them back to the camp, in which there was a great famine. And they sold one donkey's load for eight *purpurati*,[4] which would come to one hundred twenty sous in deniers. Many of our men died there because they did not have the means to buy at such high prices.

THE FLIGHT OF WILLIAM THE CARPENTER
AND PETER THE HERMIT—AROUND JANUARY 20, 1098

Then, William the Carpenter[5] and Peter the Hermit, because of this great calamity and this misery, secretly ran away. Tancred went after them, caught them, and brought them back in shame. They gave him their word and their pledge that they would freely return to the camp and ask forgiveness from the worthy lords. The whole of the night, William remained in the tent of Bohemond, lying on the earth like an evil thing.

At daybreak, he came before Bohemond, red-faced, and Bohemond said to him, "O, wretched and most dishonorable man in all of France, scoundrel and felon of all the Gauls! O most detestable of all that this earth endures! Why did you so shamefully run away? Perhaps you wanted to betray these warriors and the army of Christ, as you betrayed those others in Spain?"[6]

He kept completely quiet and not one word came out of him. Then nearly all the Frenchmen[7] gathered together and humbly asked the lord Bohemond to let him suffer no other penalty. He agreed to what they wanted and said, "I shall happily agree for the love of you, if he will swear with all his heart and all his soul that he will never abandon the path to Jerusalem, whether good or bad, and Tancred must swear that neither he nor his men shall harm him in any way." When Tancred heard these words, he freely agreed, and Bohemond sent William away. But afterward, it was not long before the Carpenter, driven by great shame, secretly fled away.[8]

Such was the poverty and misery that God reserved for us because of our sins. In the whole of the army, one could not find a thousand warriors who had kept their horses in the best condition.

THE DEPARTURE OF
TETIGUS—BEGINNING OF FEBRUARY 1098

In the meantime, Tetigus,[9] our enemy, hearing that the army of the Turks was marching against us, claimed to be filled with fear for our sake, thinking that we had all been killed or had fallen in the hands of our enemies; and making up all kinds of lies, he said: "High lords and valiant men, you see the dire hardship that we are in, and no help can come to us from any direction. So, allow me to return to Romania, my homeland, and do not be doubtful, I will make sure that ships are sent here by sea filled with grain, wine, barley, meat, flour, cheese, and all good things that are needed. I shall have sent to you horses that you can sell and will have supplies brought here by land according to the promise of the emperor. Look, I will swear before you all to be faithful and to look after everything. My people and my tent shall remain in this camp, that you may firmly believe that I shall return as quickly as I can."

Thus he ended his fine words. This enemy then went away and left all his things in the camp. But he remains and will always remain a liar.[10] We were in a very bad way: The Turks attacked us from all around so that no man dared to go beyond the tents—and so on the one hand, they were always harassing us, and on the other hand, hunger crucified us—and no help, no aid came to us. The common soldiers and those who were very poor fled to Cyprus, Romania, or into the mountains.[11]

As well, we did not dare go down to the sea for fear of those infernal Turks. There was not any road open to us.

TURKISH REINFORCEMENTS ARRIVE AT ANTIOCH—FEBRUARY 8, 1098

Consequently, when lord Bohemond heard of an innumerable multitude of Turks coming against us, he came cautiously before the others and said, "High and valiant warriors, what should we do? We are not enough in number to fight in two parts. But do you know what we might be able to do? We could divide ourselves into two groups: The foot soldiers would remain and guard the pavilions and, if they are able to, keep in check those who are inside the city. The other part, consisting of our warriors, could come out with us in front of the enemy who stays close to us in the castle of Aregh, beyond the bridge of iron."

BOHEMOND ATTACKS THE TURKS—FEBRUARY 9, 1098

When it was evening, that wise man Bohemond left the tents along with the other valiant warriors and assumed position between the river and the lake.[12] At daybreak, he ordered patrols to be quickly sent out to go and see how many cavalry squadrons the Turks had, where they were located, and indeed what they were up to. And so they headed out and carefully began to find out where the battle line of the Turks might be concealed. Then they saw innumerable Turks separated into two lines of battle and coming up from one side of the river. The larger part of their army was following behind. The patrols headed back quickly and said, "Look, look, they are coming! Everyone get ready, because they are almost on top of us!"

Then that wise man Bohemond said, "High lords and invincible warriors, take up battle formation." And they replied to him, "You are wise and valiant. You are great and magnificent. You are brave and victorious. You are an authority on battles and judge of combat. Do everything that you must. Everything depends on you. Do, and have us do, what you think best."

At that, Bohemond commanded that each leader should put his own cohort into battle order. This was done, and six battalions were created; five of these charged at the Turks. Bohemond followed behind very slowly with his own battalion. Our men effectively went into battle; one man fought hand-to-hand with another. The clamor rose to heaven, since everyone was fighting at once; the falling javelins darkened the air.

Then the greater part of their army arrived, which had been a little behind, and it attacked our men with such ferocity that they began to fall back, little by little. When he saw this, that wisest man Bohemond groaned, and then he called his constable, Robert, son of Gerard,[13] saying, "Go forward swiftly, like a brave man. Help the cause of God and of the Holy Sepulcher. And know that this battle, in reality, is not of the flesh, but of the spirit.[14] Therefore be the bravest athlete of Christ! Go in peace and may the Lord be with you always."

And shielded on all sides by the sign of the cross, and like a lion that has been hungry for three or four days who emerges roaring from his cave, and thirsting for the blood of beasts and who hurls himself suddenly upon the flock, tearing the sheep who run about here and there—such was the way in which he fell upon the flock of the Turks.[15] So fiercely did he chase them that the flaming tongues of his banner flew above the heads of Turks.[16]

The other battalions, when they saw Bohemond's banner so nobly leading onward, at once stopped falling back. Then our men altogether rushed at the Turks, who were so bewildered that they took to flight. Our men chased after them, lopping off their heads, right up to the bridge of iron.[17]

THE TURKISH REINFORCEMENTS
ARE COMPLETELY ROUTED—FEBRUARY 9, 1098

The Turks quickly fell back to their castle, gathered up everything they found there, ransacked the entire castle, set fire to it, and then fled. The Armenians and Syrians, knowing that the Turks had been completely defeated in battle, came out and waited in narrow places and killed and captured many of them.

And so, our enemies were defeated, by the will of God. Our men caught enough of the horses and other things that they badly needed.

They brought back to the city gate one hundred heads of the dead Turks, where the delegation of the emir of Babylon had set up camp,[18] which the emir had sent to our worthy lords. Those that had remained behind in the camp had spent the whole day fighting, in front of the three gates of the city, with those inside the city. This battle was fought on the Tuesday before Lent, five days before the Ides of February,[19] by the favor of our Lord Jesus Christ who with the Father and the Holy Spirit lives and reigns, God through eternity, from age to age. Amen.

Here ends the sixth book. Here begins the seventh book.

The Seventh Narrative

The Siege of Antioch Continues—March 1098

THE CRUSADERS BUILD
A CASTLE—FRIDAY, MARCH 5, 1098

$\mathcal{O}$ur men returned, by the grace of God, jubilant and joyful in the triumph they had that day. The defeated enemies, vanquished in every way, kept on fleeing, running and scurrying here and there, some going into Khorasan and others into the land of the Saracens.[1] But our leaders—seeing that our enemies inside the city were always raiding us and keeping us hemmed in day and night and looking for ways to harm us—came together as one and said, "Before we lose our men, let us build a castle at the mosque which is at the front of the city gate, where the bridge is, and thus we may be able to keep our enemies in check."[2]

They all agreed and praised it as a good thing to do. The count of Saint-Gilles was the first to speak: "Give me the help to build this castle and I shall fortify it and watch over it."

Bohemond responded, "If this is what you want, and if the others approve, I shall go with you to the port of Saint Symeon[3] and bring back safely those men that are there who know how to do such work.[4] And those that stay behind here must fortify themselves so that they can defend themselves against attacks from all sides."

And all this was done, and then the count and Bohemond left for the port of Saint Symeon.[5]

We who stayed behind got together and were beginning on the castle when the Turks got ready, emerged from the city, and came before us to fight. And they hurled themselves upon us and put our men to flight and also killed many of our men, which gave us much sorrow.

A TURKISH AMBUSH—MARCH 5–6, 1098

And the following day, when the Turks saw that our leaders were away, that they had left for the port the day before, they got ready and came out to attack those who would return from the port. And when they saw the count and Bohemond coming and leading their men, they began to grind their teeth and loudly screech and yell, as they circled around our men, hurling javelins and shooting arrows, wounding and cruelly lopping off heads. They attacked with such ferocity that our men fled into the high mountain or wherever they could find a way. Those that could flee as fast as they could did escape alive. Those who could not flee quickly enough were given death. And on that day, more than a thousand of our warriors and foot soldiers were led into martyrdom, and as we believe, they ascended into heaven and received the white stoles of the martyrs.

THE TURKS ARE DRIVEN BACK—MARCH 6, 1098

Bohemond did not take the same road as they had taken, but with a few warriors came quickly to us who were gathered as one. And we, inflamed by the slaughter of our men, and invoking the name of Christ and being confident in our hope of reaching the Holy Sepulcher, went forward together to fight them, and we fell upon them with one heart and spirit. Our enemies, and God's, just stood there bewildered and stunned. They had thought of defeating us and killing us as they had with the men of the count and of Bohemond. But God the Almighty did not allow this to happen. Thus, the warriors of the true God, armed with the sign of the cross, charged at them quickly and bravely attacked them, and they hurriedly fled from the middle of the narrow bridge to the entrance of the city.[6] Those who could not cross over the bridge, because of the great stampede of men and horses, met eternal death along with the devil and his angels.[7]

And so we got the better of them and pushed them into the river. The swift current of the river was seen to be made red by the blood of the Turks, and if one of them tried to climb up the posts of the bridge, or tried to swim to the bank, he was struck down by our men who stood all along the bank of the river. The shouts and clamor of our men and theirs resounded up to heaven. The rain of javelins and arrows hid the sky and the brightness of the day. And when the Christian women of the city came to the windows in the walls and saw the miserable fate of the Turks, they secretly clapped their hands. The Armenians and the Syrians, by order of the leader of the Turks, had to shoot arrows and missiles at us, either willingly or by force. Twelve emirs of the Turks lost their bodies and their souls in this battle, along with others of their bravest and strongest warriors who were considered the best of those fighting to defend the city and who numbered one thousand five hundred. Those others who remained alive no longer had the courage to shriek and cry out as they once used to do day and night. It was night alone which came and separated everyone, us and them, and night alone stopped the fighting, the spear thrust, the sword cut, the arrow shot. Thus were our enemies defeated by the power of God and by the Holy Sepulcher, and henceforth, they no longer had the same courage, either in word or in deed, as they had before. And on that day, we greatly recovered supplies which were enough for our needs, and especially horses.

THE TURKS TRY TO BURY THEIR DEAD—MARCH 7, 1098

The next day, at dawn, other Turks came out of the city and collected all the stinking corpses of the dead Turks that they found along the bank of the river. They buried them at the mosque located beyond the bridge and in front of the city gate. And they buried with them cloaks, bezants, gold, bows, arrows, and many other objects whose names we do not know. When our men heard that the Turks had buried their dead in this way, they got ready and came in all haste to that diabolical building[8] and commanded that the corpses be dug up, the graves destroyed, and the corpses be dragged from their tombs. All the corpses were tossed into a pit, and their heads were cut off and carried to our tents, so that the exact number of the dead could be determined—except for those that they loaded onto four horses belonging to messengers of the emir of Babylonia, and these they sent toward the sea.[9] When the Turks saw this, they were seized by pain and grieved nearly to death. And each day they lamented and did nothing other than weep and shriek.

THE CRUSADERS BUILD A CASTLE—MARCH 8–19, 1098

On the third day, we came together and greatly rejoiced to build the castle, mentioned above, with stones which we dug up from the tombs of the Turks.[10] When the castle was finished, we began to put pressure on our enemies from all sides whose pride had already been reduced to nothing. And so we walked about safely, here and there, up to the gate and to the mountains, praising and glorifying our God to whom be honor and glory from age to age. Amen.

Here ends the seventh book. Here begins the eighth book.

The Eighth Narrative

March to June 1098

THE TURKS ARE CONTAINED—MID-MARCH 1098

$\mathscr{B}$y this time, all paths were blockaded and cut off for the Turks, except for that part of the river where the castle and the monastery stood.[1] If we could fortify this castle with sufficient force, none of them would dare to leave by the city gate. Then our men took counsel and spoke with one, unified voice: "Let us choose from one among us to bravely guard the castle and hinder our enemies from going into the mountain and the plain, and not let them enter or leave the city."

TANCRED MAKES AN AGREEMENT—APRIL 5, 1098

Tancred was the first to come before them, and he said: "If I know what reward I shall get, I shall alertly guard the castle with my men alone. And I shall manfully block the path which our enemies use to attack us so often."

And they promised to give him four hundred marks of silver. And Tancred wasted no time but left with his warriors and foot soldiers and immediately obstructed the paths of the Turks so that none of them, so struck were they by terror, dared to come out of the city gate, either for hay, or for wood, or for anything that they needed. Tancred remained there with his men and began to cordon off the city completely.

The same day a great many Armenians and Syrians came through the mountains all in one piece, bringing provisions for the Turks to supply the city. Tancred came out to stop them and captured them, along with all that they had brought, namely grain, wine, barley, oil, and other things of this sort. And so in this way, Tancred demonstrated his strength and succeeded so very well in blocking the paths and cutting off the Turks until Antioch was captured.

I cannot narrate everything that we did before the capture of this city. Indeed, no one found in this area, whether a priest or a layman, can possibly write down, or narrate, all the things that were done. But I shall try to tell you just a little bit.[2]

BOHEMOND MAKES A FRIEND—END OF MAY 1098

There was a certain emir, a Turk by lineage, whose name was Pyrrhus[3] and who had become a great friend of Bohemond.[4] Now, Bohemond often sent messengers to him inside the city, urging him to accept his friendship and promising him that he would gladly have him enter Christianity and that he would heap on him many riches and great honor. Pyrrhus agreed to these words and these promises and said, "I have three towers in my custody. I promise them to him, and I shall receive him in them at whatever hour he chooses."

And so having found a way to enter inside the city, Bohemond rejoiced, and then with a peaceful mind and calm face, he came before all the other chief lords, and said: "Warriors, bravest of men, you see how we are all in utter poverty and misery, both lords and commoners, and we do not know from which quarter help will come to us. Therefore, if you think it good and honorable, let one of us be placed above all others, and if that man can manage to capture the city, either through his own ability or by assault, by himself or through others, let us agree with one voice to give the city to him."

All the others refused and opposed him, saying: "No one will get possession of the city, but we shall all have equal possession of it. We have all worked equally, and so we must all have equal honor."

When Bohemond heard these words, he smiled to himself and quickly left.

BOHEMOND IS PROMISED ANTIOCH—MAY 29, 1098

Not long afterward, we got word of an army of our enemies: Turks, Paulicians, Azymites,[5] and many other nations. At once all our leaders came together and took counsel, and said: "If Bohemond can get the city by himself, or through others, we shall happily give it to him, with the stipulation that if the emperor comes to our aid and fulfills all the conditions that he promised and swore to give us, by right we shall let him have the city: otherwise, Bohemond shall take possession of it."

Soon, Bohemond humbly began to ask his friend every day, promising humbly, greatly, and sweetly in such fashion as this: "You see how the right time has come for us to accomplish the good work that we had agreed upon. Therefore, help me, Pyrrhus, my friend." He was very pleased by this and said that he would help him in every way he could, as he said he would.

When the next night came, he sent his own son as a pledge to Bohemond to confirm that the entrance to the city would be secured. And he also sent word that at dawn Bohemond should summon all the men of the Franks, pretending to head out to raid the land of the Saracens,[6] and then to quickly return through the mountain to the right.[7]

"And then I shall," he said, "keep a careful watch for these troops and shall receive them into the towers that I have in my power to guard."

ANTIOCH IS TAKEN—JUNE 3, 1098

Then Bohemond quickly sent for one of his foot soldiers, Malacorona by name,[8] and ordered him to go as a herald and muster a great army of the Franks and get them to prepare diligently to go into the land of the Saracens. And he did as he was ordered.

Next Bohemond entrusted his strategy to Duke Godfrey and to the count of Flanders, and also to the count of Saint-Gilles and to the bishop of Puy, saying to them: "By the favor of God's grace, Antioch will be delivered to us this night."

And then everything was made ready: The warriors held the plain and the foot soldiers held the mountains. The whole night they marched and they rode, right until dawn which is when they drew near to the towers, whose custodian had been watching the entire night. Hurriedly Bohemond dismounted and instructed everyone, saying, "Go forward with untroubled minds and joyful unity and climb up the ladder into Antioch, which we shall quickly take, if it pleases God, into our care."

They came to the ladder which was erected and firmly tied to the city walls, and almost sixty of our men climbed up and took possession of the towers that were under his custody. But when Pyrrhus saw that so very few of our men had come up, he began to get nervous, and he began to fear that both he and our men would fall into the hands of the Turks. And he said, "*Micro Francos echome* (that is, We have very few Franks).[9] Where is that fervent Bohemond? Where is that invincible man?"

And so a Langobard[10] foot soldier quickly descended and quickly ran to Bohemond, saying, "O brave man, why are you just standing there? What did you come here to get? Look, we have already taken three towers."

Then he and the others marshaled themselves and they all joyfully advanced to the ladders. And those who were in the towers by now shouted in a joyful voice: "*Deus le volt!* God wills it!" And we shouted up the same thing.

And so they began the marvelous ascent; they climbed up and swiftly ran to the other towers. They killed all those they found inside. And in this way was the brother of Pyrrhus killed. In the meantime, the ladder by which our men were climbing up broke, and this plunged us into deep anxiety and sorrow. Though the ladder broke, there was close by to the left of us a certain door, which was shut and which was not noticed by some of us, because it was still night. But we felt and prodded about for it, and having located it, we all ran at it, broke it down, and got inside.

Then, a great uproar of innumerable people echoed throughout the whole city. But Bohemond wasted no time with this and ordered that his glorious banner be planted on a hill opposite the citadel.[11] Everyone inside the city was shouting at once.

When dawn broke, those who were still inside their tents heard the great clamor which arose from the city. As they ran out, they saw Bohemond's banner on the hill, and they dashed as fast as they could and entered the city through the gates and killed the Turks and the Saracens that they found there, except for those who escaped by running up to the citadel. And some of the Turks fled through the gates and in this way they got away alive. Now Cassian,[12] their leader, was also among those who fled, and he took with him his followers. And as they fled they came into the land of Tancred,[13] not far from the city. Their horses were completely worn out, and so they entered a *casal*[14] and hid in a house. But the inhabitants of those mountains, namely, Syrians and Armenians, recognized them, and they captured him and lopped off his head and brought it to Bohemond in order to purchase their freedom. His sword belt and scabbard were worth sixty bezants.[15]

All these things happened on the third day of June, on the fifth feast day, three days before the Nones of June.[16] All the places of the city were full of dead bodies, so that no one could stay there because of the stench. Indeed, no one could move about in the streets without stepping on the bodies of the dead.

Here ends the eighth book. Here begins the ninth book.

The Ninth Narrative

June 1098

CURBARAM ARRIVES AT ANTIOCH—JUNE 4, 1098

Curbaram,[1] leader of the army of the sultan of Persia,[2] while still in Khorasan, had received a messenger from Cassian, emir of Antioch, asking for help at an opportune time, as he was being badly besieged in Antioch by the very powerful Franks; and if Curbaram sent him aid, Cassian would give him the city of Antioch, or at the least a great amount of money. Now Curbaram had already gathered a large army of Turks, which he had been assembling for a long time, and he had also been given permission to kill Christians by the caliph, their pope.[3] And so he at once began the long march toward Antioch. The emir of Jerusalem came to help him with his army;[4] the king of Damascus came with a great many of his men.[5] And so Curbaram gathered innumerable pagan men, namely Turks, Arabs, Saracens, Paulicians, Azymites, Kurds, Persians, Agulani, and many other innumerable men. And the Agulani numbered three thousand; they fear neither lance, nor arrow, nor any other weapon, because they and their horses are entirely covered in iron and they themselves carry no weapons into combat other than swords. And all of them came to besiege Antioch and to scatter the gathered Franks.

And as they came close to the city, they met Sensadolus,[6] the son of Cassian the emir of Antioch. He ran up to Curbaram, and with tears implored him, saying, "Invincible prince, I am a suppliant begging you to help me because the Franks have completely besieged me in Antioch, and they hold the city in their power. They want to chase us from the region of Romania, from Syria, and even from Khorasan. They have gotten all that they wanted. They killed my father. Nothing further remains for them to do but to kill me and you and all others of our race. I have been expecting your help for a long time now that you would rescue me from this peril."

And Curbaram replied, "If you want me to search with all my heart for ways to help you and to truly rescue you from this peril, place the citadel in my hands and you shall see what kind of help I give you, for I will guard it with my own men."

Then Sensadolus replied, "If you can kill all the Franks and then send me their heads, I shall give you the citadel, and I shall do you homage, and I shall guard this citadel faithfully for you."

And Curbaram said, "No, not at all. Rather, place the castle[7] in my hands at once."

And so, for better or for worse, Sensadolus gave him the castle.[8]

On the third day after our entry into the city, their advance guard appeared before the walls of the city, and their army set up camp at the bridge of iron; and they took one of the towers and killed all those they found inside, so that none escaped alive, except their leader, whom we found later, bound in chains of iron, after the great battle.

CURBARAM LAYS SIEGE TO ANTIOCH—JUNE 5, 1098

The next day, the pagan army was on the march, and when it approached the city, it camped between the two rivers[9] and stayed there for two days. After taking charge of the castle,[10] Curbaram summoned one of his emirs, whom he knew to be truthful, gentle, and peaceful, and he said to him, "In trustworthiness to me, I want you to guard this castle,[11] because I have known for a long time of your loyalty, and so I adjure you to guard this citadel[12] with great care."

The emir said to him, "I would never want to agree to such a request, but I will do it on this condition, if the Franks drive you back in mortal combat and they are victorious, I shall at once surrender this castle to them."

And Curbaram said to him, "I know of your honesty and bravery, and I will agree to everything you think is good to do."

Then Curbaram returned to his army. Now the Turks, wishing to make fun of the army of the Franks, brought a cheap sword all covered with rust, a really bad wooden bow, and a spear that was completely useless for Curbaram to have a look at; these they had snatched from the poor pilgrims. And they said to him, "Look at the weapons the Franks have brought to fight us."

Curbaram laughed and said in the presence of everyone, "Such are the ferocious and brilliant weapons that the Christians have brought to conquer us in Asia and with which they confidently think of chasing us beyond the farthest reaches of Khorasan, and to erase our name beyond the rivers of the Amazons,[13] they who drove out all our parents from Romania and from Antioch, the royal city, which is the praiseworthy capital of all Syria."

Right away he summoned his scribe and said to him, "As quickly as possible, write charters which may be read in Khorasan, namely: 'To the Caliph our pope and to the lord sultan our king, warriors most valiant, and all the bravest warriors of Khorasan, greetings and highest honor. Satisfy yourselves joyfully, and with a festive resolve, fill your stomachs. And let commands be given and announcements made in all the region for everyone to give free rein to their passion and their lust and by this pleasure conceive many sons who shall fight bravely against the Christians. Now gladly accept these three weapons which we have snatched away from a group of Franks and from them learn what kinds of weapons the Frankish men have brought to overcome us. Let everyone also know that I have all the Franks locked up right inside Antioch, and that I hold the citadel in my power; they are down below in the city. I have them now all in my hands, and they will be either given the capital sentence or led to Khorasan in wretched captivity, because they threatened us and wanted to drive us back with their weapons and chase us out of our borders, as they chased out our parents from Romania and from Syria. Also, I swear to you by Mohamed and by all our gods[14] that I shall not again present myself before you until I have taken by the strength of my right hand the royal city of Antioch, and all of Syria and Romania, and Bulgaria,[15] right up to Apulia,[16] in honor of the gods, and of you, and of all who are of the race of the Turks."

This was the end of his message.

THE FOREBODING OF CURBARAM'S MOTHER

Now, the mother of this very same Curbaram, who was in the city of Aleppo,[17] came to him quickly and said to him, "Son, is it true what I have heard?"

And he said, "What?"

And she said, "I have heard that you want to fight against the Frankish people."

He said, "Yes, you should know that it is all true."

She said, "I beg you, son, in the name of all the gods, and by your own great goodness, do not enter into a battle against the Franks, because you are an unbeatable warrior. No one has ever seen you being chased off the battlefield by a conqueror. Your toughness is well known, and brave warriors tremble whenever they hear your name. We know already, son, how mighty you are in war, and how brave and how wise in the ways of war. No people, Christian or pagan, can show any courage before you, but they run away as soon as they hear your name, like sheep fleeing before a raging lion.[18] For these reasons, dearest son, listen to my advice and never even entertain the possibility, in your mind or in your councils, of starting a war against the Christian people."[19]

When Curbaram had heard these maternal warnings, he responded with insolent words: "What is this that you are telling me, mother? Are you insane or completely crazy? I have more emirs than there are Christians, either great or small."

His mother responded to him,[20] "O sweetest son, the Christians cannot wage battle against you. I know that they are incapable of fighting us. But their God fights for them each day; day and night He defends them by His protection, and He watches over them like a shepherd watches over his flock, and He does not permit them to be harmed or troubled by any nation whatsoever. And those that want to oppose them, their God confounds, as He said through the mouth of the prophet David: '*Scatter the nations that delight in wars.*'[21] And furthermore: '*Pour out thy wrath upon the nations that know thee not, And upon the kingdoms that call not upon thy name.*'[22] Now, before they can even prepare to start a battle, their God, Almighty and Invincible, along with His saints, has already vanquished all their enemies. How much greater will He do to you who are His enemy and you who have prepared to oppose Him with all your courage? Dearest one, in all truth, understand also that these Christians are called the '*sons of Christ*,'[23] and by the mouths of the prophets, '*the sons of adoption and of promise*,'[24] and by the apostle, 'they are the heirs of Christ.'[25] It is to them that Christ has already given the inheritance which He promised, saying through the prophets: '*From the rising of the sun to its going down shall be your boundaries, and no man shall stand against you.*'[26] Who can contradict these words, or oppose them? Indeed, if you start this battle against them, great will be your loss and great your shame. You will lose many of your faithful warriors, and you will leave behind all your plunder which you have gathered together, and, ruined, you will flee in terror. You will not die in this battle, but you will die this very year, because this God does not at once judge the offender who has stirred Him to anger, but whenever He wants to, He punishes him with obvious vengeance. And so I fear that He will judge you severely. You will not die, I say, but you shall lose all that you possess right now."

And then Curbaram was terribly grief stricken deep inside, and when he had heard his mother's words, he replied: "Dearest mother, I beg you, who told you these things about the Christian people, that their God loves them so much, and that He has within Himself such great strength in combat, that these Christians will conquer us in the battle for Antioch, and that they will capture our plunder, and that they will chase us away after a great victory, and that this very year I shall die a quick death?"

Then his mother replied with sorrow: "Dearest son, look, more than a hundred years ago it was discovered in our book[27] and in the volumes of the gentiles that the Christian people will attack us and will completely conquer us and reign over the pagans, and our people everywhere will submit to them. But I do not know if all these things will happen now or in the future. Indeed, filled with grief, I followed you to Aleppo, that beautiful city, where, through careful study and observation, I read the stars in the sky and carefully scrutinized the planets and the twelve signs, and the innumerable oracles. In all these, I read that the Christian people shall conquer us completely, and I fear for you greatly, in my exceeding sorrow, that I shall lose you."[28]

Curbaram said to her: "Dearest mother, tell me all those things which my heart will not let me believe."

And in reply she said, "That I shall willingly do, dearest, if you will tell me what things you do not understand."

And he said to her: "Now, are not Bohemond and Tancred the gods of the Franks, and do they not deliver them from their enemies, for do they not eat two thousand cows and four thousand pigs at a single meal?"[29]

The mother replied, "Dearest son, Bohemond and Tancred are mortals, like everyone else, but their God greatly loves them above all others, and he gives them the courage to fight those before them; for their God, Almighty is His name,[30] made the heaven and earth and the deep sea and all that is in them;[31] whose throne is prepared in heaven from eternity,[32] whose might is to be feared everywhere."[33]

The son said, "Be that as it may, I shall not hold back from fighting them."

And when his mother heard that he would not listen to her advice, she returned to Aleppo, filled with sadness, but not without taking with her all the plunder that she could carry.[34]

CURBARAM'S FIRST ENCOUNTER WITH THE CRUSADERS—JUNE 5, 1098

Now on the third day, Curbaram armed himself, and a large part of the Turks came with him to the city, from that part where the castle stood.[35] And, thinking that we could resist them, we began to get ready to fight, but their strength was so great that we could not hold them back and we were pushed back into the city, the door to which was so narrow and confined that many were crushed to death by others.

DESERTIONS—JUNE 10, 1098

On that fifth feast day,[36] some fought outside and some fought inside the city, for the entire day right into evening. It was at this point that William of Grandmesnil,[37] Alberic his brother,[38] Guy Trousseau,[39] and Lambert the Poor,[40] who had been terrified by the battle of the day before which had also lasted until evening, fled by secretly going down the wall at night and ran on foot to the sea, so that their feet and their hands were worn right down to the bone. And there were many others, whose names I do not know, who fled with them.[41] When they got to the ships which were in the port of Saint Symeon, they said to the sailors, "You wretches, what are you doing here? All those who were with us are dead, and we ourselves have barely escaped death, and the army of the Turks is besieging the others in the city." When they heard this, they stood dazed, struck with terror; and they ran to the ships and headed for the sea. Then the Turks fell upon them, killing those that they found and burning the ships that were at the mouth of the river, and they carried away plunder.

As for us who remained behind,[42] we could not bear the weight of their arms, and so we made a wall between us and them, which we guarded day and night.[43] All this while, so horrible was our torment that we began to devour our horses and our donkeys.[44]

A PRIEST'S VISION—JUNE 11, 1098

One day, our leaders, filled with sorrow and pain, were standing in the upper part of the city, in front of the citadel, when a priest[45] came before them and said, "High lords, if it pleases you, listen to this thing that I have seen in a vision. One night I lay face down in the church of Saint Mary, the Mother of our Lord Jesus Christ, when there appeared before me the Savior of the world, along with His mother and Saint Peter, prince of apostles, and He stood before me and said, 'Do you know me?' To which I responded, 'No.' When I said this, behold, a cross appeared above His head. And the Lord asked me again, saying, 'Do you know me?' And I said to him, 'I would not recognize you were it not for a cross above your head that I see resembling that of our Savior's.' And he said, 'I am He.' At once I fell at His feet, pleading humbly to help us in our torment that had come over us. The Lord replied, 'I have already helped you very well, and I will help you again. I allowed you to seize Nicaea, and I have led you here. I have shared in the misery that you suffered during the siege of Antioch. Behold, I gave you opportune help and brought you safe and sound inside the city. But behold you have given yourself over to perverse lusts with Christian and depraved pagan women, from which a great stench rises up to heaven.' Then the kind Virgin and Saint Peter fell at His feet, and they pleaded with Him and prayed Him to help His people in this tribulation. And Saint Peter said to Him, 'Lord, for a long time have the pagan people held my house, in which they have done many appallingly evil things. And now, Lord, the enemies have been driven out and there is rejoicing among the angels in heaven.' And the Lord said to me, 'Go, therefore, and tell my people to return to me and I shall return to them. In five days, I will send them a great help. And let them daily sing the entire response, *They are assembled*, along with the verse.'[46] High lords, if you do not believe that this is true, allow me to climb up this tower and I shall throw myself down. If I am unhurt, then believe this to be true. And if I am hurt and injured, then lop off my head and throw me into the fire.'"

Then the bishop of Puy commanded that the Gospels and the crucifix be brought so that he might swear to the truth of all this. Then all our leaders took counsel and swore a sacred oath that none among them would flee, either for fear of death or to save his life. They say that the first to swear was Bohemond, then the count of Saint Gilles, and then Robert the Norman, Duke Godfrey, and the count of Flanders. Indeed, Tancred even swore and promised that as long as he had forty warriors with him, he would not turn away from this battle, nor would he turn away from the road to Jerusalem. When the gathered Christians heard of this sacred oath, they were very happy.

THE HOLY LANCE—AFTER JUNE 10, 1098

There was a certain pilgrim in our army, whose name was Peter,[47] and to whom, before we entered the city, there appeared Saint Andrew the Apostle; and he said to him, "What are you doing, good man?" And Peter replied to him, "And you, who are you?" The Apostle said to him, "I am Andrew the Apostle. Know this, my son, that when you enter the city and if you go to the church of Saint Peter,[48] you will find there the lance of our Savior Jesus Christ with which He was pierced when He hung upon the cross." After saying all this, the Apostle disappeared.

Now this pilgrim was afraid to reveal the advice of the Apostle, and so he did not tell our pilgrims. He thought he had seen a vision. And he said, "Lord, who will believe it?" At that very hour, Saint Andrew took him and carried him to that place where the lance was hidden in the ground. And again during the time when we were in that situation mentioned above, Saint Andrew came back and said to him, "Why have you not taken the lance from the ground, as I told you? You should know that whoever carries this lance into battle shall never be defeated by the enemy."

Then, right away, Peter revealed to us the mystery of the Apostle—but the people did not believe him and pushed him away, saying, "How can we believe such a thing?" They were all frightened, for they thought themselves close to death. But he came and swore that it was the complete and utter truth, that Saint Andrew had appeared to him twice in a vision and had said to him, "Rise up, go, and say to the people of God to not be afraid, but to firmly believe with all their heart in the one true God, and they shall be triumphant everywhere. In five days, the Lord shall send a message which shall fill them with joy and with cheer. And so if they want to fight, as soon as they head out all together to battle, all their enemies will be defeated and none shall stand against them." Now when they heard that their enemies were all going to be destroyed, they began to take heart and they comforted each other, saying, "Let us rise up and let us be brave and courageous in all ways, because soon God will come to help us, and there will be a great consolation for His people upon whom He has looked during their affliction."[49]

THE TURKS ATTACK—JUNE 11, 1098

Then the Turks, who were up in the castle,[50] fell upon us so brutally from all sides that one day they managed to trap three of our warriors inside the tower that stood in front of their castle,[51] for the pagans had burst out with such force that we could not withstand the impact. Two of the warriors came out of the tower wounded, but the third manfully defended himself the whole day against the attack of the Turks, and on that day he struck down two Turks at the wall, after breaking his lances—on that day three lances broke in his hands, but both Turks got the capital sentence. His name was Hugh the Mad, from the army of Gosfred of Monte Scabioso.[52]

BOHEMOND BURNS ANTIOCH—JUNE 12, 1098

Now when that venerable man Bohemond saw that he could not make his men come out to the citadel and fight—because they lay trembling in houses, some from hunger, others from fear of the Turks—he was very angry, and ordered that the city be put to the torch, around the area where Cassian's palace was located. Seeing this, those that were inside the city abandoned their houses and all their possessions and fled, some toward the citadel,[53] some to the gate held by the count of Saint Gilles, and others to the gate held by Duke Godfrey, each one to his own people. And then there suddenly arose a great tempest of wind, so that no one could stand up straight. And then that wise man, Bohemond, grew very worried, because he feared for the churches of Saint Peter and Saint Mary, and the other churches. This furor lasted from the third hour until midnight—and so two thousand churches and houses were burned.[54] And it came about that by the middle of the night all the violence of the fire suddenly died down.

A PORTENT IN THE NIGHT SKY—JUNE 13–14, 1098

The Turks in the castle,[55] inside the city, fought with our men day and night, and it was only because of our weapons that we could hold them at bay. When our men saw that they could not put up with this for much longer—because he who had bread could not eat it and he that had any water could not drink it[56]—they made a wall of stone and lime between us and them, and they built a castle and catapults for security.[57] One group of Turks remained inside the citadel and fought us; another group was encamped in a valley near the citadel.[58]

Indeed, that very night, a fire appeared in the sky, coming from the west, and it advanced and fell upon the army of the Turks, to the great amazement of our men and of the Turks.[59] In the morning, the frightened Turks all fled, scared by the fire, and they came to the gate held by lord Bohemond, where they set up camp. But those inside the citadel continued to fight our men day and night, shooting arrows, wounding and killing. The remaining Turks continued to besiege the city on all sides, so that none of our men dared to leave or enter except secretly and at night. Yes, indeed, we were besieged and tormented by them, whose numbers were countless.

TIME OF PRIVATION—JUNE 14–28, 1098

These profane ones, and these enemies of God, kept us so closely sealed up inside the city of Antioch that many died of hunger, for a small loaf of bread cost one bezant, and there is no use talking about the wine. Men ate and sold the flesh of horses and donkeys; a chicken cost fifteen sous,[60] eggs two sous, and a walnut cost one denier. Everything was so expensive. They cooked and ate the leaves of figs, vines, and thistles, and all other trees, so terrible was the famine. Still others cooked and ate the dried skins of horses, of camels, of cows, and even buffaloes. This great discomfort and these great hardships we suffered for the name of Christ and to keep free the road to the Holy Sepulcher. Such was the suffering, such the famine and the terror that we endured for twenty-six days.

THE COWARDICE OF STEPHEN OF CHARTRES—JUNE 14–20, 1098

Now, just before Antioch was taken, that fool, Stephen of Chartres,[61] whom all our leaders had elected as our chief commander, pretended to have caught some disease and shamefully went off to another fortified city called Alexandretta.[62] And when we were shut up in the city with no one to come and save us, we waited for him every day to come and help us. But when he heard that the army of the Turks had surrounded us and had besieged us, he secretly came up along a neighboring mountain which was close to Antioch and saw the countless number of tents. Fear took hold of him, and he retreated and quickly fled with his army. He returned to his camp, gathered everything up, and quickly beat a hasty retreat.

Afterward, when he came before the emperor at Philomelium,[63] he asked to speak to him personally, and said to him secretly, "You should know that Antioch really has been taken, but the citadel has not fallen. Our men are badly besieged and most likely have already been killed by the Turks. Go back, therefore, as fast as you can, so that they might not find you and these men that you lead."

Then, the emperor, shaking with terror, secretly summoned Guy,[64] the brother of Bohemond, and some others, and said to them, "High lords, what should we do? Behold, all our men are shut in and badly besieged, and maybe at this very hour they have been killed by the hands of the Turks or led off into captivity, as this miserable count, who shamefully fled, has just described. If you want, we can quickly turn back and beat a hasty retreat, so that we will not die a sudden death, as the others have died."

When Guy, that most honorable warrior, heard such lies, he began to weep, as well as the others, and to grieve loudly,[65] and they all with one voice said, "O true God, Three in One, why have You allowed such things to happen? Why have You permitted the people that follow You to fall into the hands of their enemies, and why have You forsaken so quickly those who wanted to liberate the road to the Holy Sepulcher? Indeed, if the word that we have heard from these rogues is true, we and all other Christians shall forsake You, and not one among us will ever again dare to invoke Your name." So bitter was this news to all the army that none among them, bishop, abbot, priest, nor layman, dared to invoke the name of Christ for several days.[66]

And no one could console Guy, who wept and beat his breast and twisted the fingers of his hands, and said, "O, my lord Bohemond, honor and ornament of the world, whom the world feared and loved. Ah, how sad I am. I was not worthy, much to my sorrow, to see your most admirable face, though I wanted nothing more. Who will give me the chance to die for you, my dearest friend and my lord? Why did I not die at once when I was taken out of my mother's womb? Why did I live to see this miserable day? Why did I not drown in the sea? Why did I not fall from my horse and break my neck? If only I had received blessed martyrdom with you, that I might have seen your most glorious end."

And when they all ran to him that they might console him and bring an end to his mourning, he took a hold of himself and said, "Do you really believe this grizzled and foolish warrior? I have never heard of any deed that he has done in the army—only that he disgracefully and shamefully retreated just like a most miserable scoundrel. And you should know that whatever he says will be a lie."[67]

In the meanwhile, the emperor commanded his men, saying, "Go and bring all the men of this land into Bulgaria. Run through the country and destroy everything everywhere, so that when the Turks come, they will have nothing at all." For better or for worse, our men turned back and retreated, grieving bitterly even unto death. Many pilgrims who were sick died because they lacked the strength to follow the army, and so they remained by the wayside and died. All the rest turned back to Constantinople.

DISCOVERY OF THE HOLY LANCE—EVENING, JUNE 14, 1098

Now we who had heard the speeches of him who had given us the message of Christ through the words of the Apostle—we made our way in all haste to the place in the church of Saint Peter, which he had described. Thirteen men dug from morning to evening, until that man found the lance, as he had indicated.[68] And they accepted it with great joy and with also fear, and a great joy arose in the entire city.

AN EMBASSY TO THE TURKS—JUNE 27, 1098

From that time on, we held among ourselves a war council. All our leaders then took counsel and resolved to send a messenger to the Turks, the enemies of Christ, that he might ask them precisely and clearly, through an interpreter, asking them why, in their pride, they had entered into Christian land, and why they had established their camp there, and why they were terrifying and slaughtering the servants of Christ. When they had finished these words, they found certain men, Peter called the Hermit and Herluin,[69] and this is what they all said to them, "Go to the damned army of the Turks and tell them all this, and ask them why in their audacity and their pride they are in the land of the Christians which is also ours."

With these words, the messengers withdrew and went into the assembly of the despicable, delivering to Curbaram and all the others the entire message: "Our leaders and our senior lords are thoroughly amazed that, filled with insolence and pride, you have entered into the land of the Christians, which is also ours. We think and believe that perhaps that you have come here that you might all become Christians, or perhaps you have come to abuse the Christians in all ways possible. Therefore, our leaders altogether ask you to quickly leave the land of God and of the Christians, which Saint Peter the Apostle converted long ago by his preaching. But they will still permit you to take all you have, namely horses and mules and donkeys, and camels, oxen, and cows, and all other possessions, and take them away wherever you want to."

Then Curbaram, the prince of the army of the sultan of Persia, and all the others, being filled with pride, replied with these fierce words, "We do not want your God or your Christianity. We do not care for them at all. We reject them completely, and at the same time we reject you. We have come here because we are greatly astonished that the leaders and chief lords that you mention call their own a land which we took away from an effeminate people. Do you want to know what we wish to tell you? Go back quickly and tell your chief lords that if they will become Turks and renounce their God whom you adore on bended knee, as well as your laws, we shall give them this land and still many others besides, along with cities and castles, so that none of you shall remain a foot soldier, but all of you shall be warriors as we are, and we shall always hold them in high friendship. Otherwise, they should know that they shall all suffer the capital sentence, or be led away in chains to Khorasan, and into perpetual captivity, serving us and our children forever and ever."[70]

And our messengers quickly came back and reported everything that these cruel people had told them. It is said that Herluin, who knew both languages, served as interpreter to Peter the Hermit.[71] During this time, our army lived in fear, not knowing what to do—on the one hand they were stricken by excruciating famine, and on the other they were tormented by the fear of the Turks.

THE CRUSADERS PREPARE THEMSELVES—JUNE 27, 1098

And then finally, after three days of fasting and of going in procession from one church to another, everyone made confession of their sins, and once absolved, faithfully received in communion the Body and Blood of Christ. And then they gave alms and had masses celebrated.

Then six battle lines were formed of those who were inside the city. Now, in the first battle line, namely at the head were Hugh Magnus, along with the Franks and the count of Flanders. In the second was Godfrey and his followers. In the third was Robert the Norman with his warriors. In the fourth was the bishop of Puy, who carried with him the lance of the Savior,[72] along with his men and with the men of Raymond, count of Saint-Gilles, who remained on the hill to guard the castle, for fear of the Turks that they might not descend into the city.[73] In the fifth battle line was Tancred, the son of the Marquis, along with his men. And indeed, in the sixth was that wise man, Bohemond, with his followers. Our bishops and priests and clerks and monks put on their holy vestments and led us out with crosses, praying and pleading with the Lord to save us and to protect us from all evil. Others stood on walls of the gate, holding holy crosses in their hands, making the sign of the Cross and blessing us. And so we got into formation, and protected by the sign of the Cross, we went out by the gate that is in front of the mosque.[74]

THE BATTLE FOR ANTIOCH—JUNE 28, 1098

When Curbaram saw the battle lines of the Franks in such good formation coming out one after the other, he said, "Let them come out, and we shall have them in our power all the better." But when they had all come outside the city, and Curbaram saw just how many the men of the Franks were, he was afraid. Then right away he commanded his emir,[75] who oversaw everything, that if he saw fire lit in front of the army, he should at once get the entire army to retreat, because he would know that the Turks had lost the battle.

And then immediately, Curbaram began to retreat little-by-little over toward the mountain, while our men followed after him. Then the Turks divided: One section went over toward the sea, while the other stayed where it was, hoping to surround our men between them. When our men saw this, they followed suit—they created a seventh battle line from the battle lines of Duke Godfrey and the count of Normandy.

Rainald was made its leader.[76] This battle line was sent out against the Turks who were coming from the sea. The Turks began to fight them and killed many of our men with arrows. Other squadrons were lined up in between the river and the mountain, over a space of two miles. These squadrons began to advance from both sides and surrounded our men, wounding with arrows and javelins.

A HOLY VISION—JUNE 28, 1098

And then there was seen, coming from the mountain, an immense army, mounted on white horses, and their banners were also white. When our men saw this army, they did not recognize it, for they did not know whose men these were. Then they understood that this was the very help sent by Christ; and the leaders were Saint George, Saint Mercurius, and Saint Demetrius.[77] This testimony is the truth, because many of our men saw it.[78]

VICTORY AT ANTIOCH—JUNE 28, 1098

Then the Turks who were coming from the side of the sea saw that they could not hold on much longer, and so they set fire to the grass, so that those who were in the tents might see it and flee. And those ones knew the signal, and they snatched up all their valuable things and fled. Now, our men were slowly advancing, fighting their way forward to where most of the army of the Turks was, namely out toward their tents. Duke Godfrey and the count of Flanders and Hugh Magnus rode out by the river bank, where most of the army of the Turks was. And they were the first, protected by the sign of the Cross, to lead a concerted attack upon them. Seeing this, the other battle lines likewise attacked them. Then the Persians and the Turks shouted, while we, calling out to the true and living God, rode out against them, beginning the battle in the name of Jesus Christ and the Holy Sepulcher. With God's help we crushed them.

Indeed, the Turks ran away in terror, and our men chased after them, right up to their tents. And the warriors of Christ desired to pursue them more than to stop for plunder, and they chased after them right up to the bridge of iron, and on the other side, right up to Tancred's castle. And they abandoned their pavilions, and their gold and silver and many furnishings, as well as their sheep and oxen, horses and mules, camels and donkeys, grain and wine, flour and many other things which they needed. The Armenians and the Syrians, who lived in the region, heard that we had overcome the Turks, and they ran to the mountain to stop them, and whomever they found from among them, they killed. And then we returned to the city with great joy, praising and blessing God, who had given victory to His people.

When the emir, who was guarding the citadel, saw Curbaram and the rest running away from the army of the Franks, he was very much afraid. At once he hurried out to ask for some Frankish banners. And so the count of Saint-Gilles, who was posted in front of the citadel, ordered that his own banner be given to him. He took that and quickly put it up on the tower. But the Longobards[79] who were positioned there at once said, "This is not Bohemond's banner." He then asked them and said, "Whose is it?" And they replied, "The count of Saint-Gilles'." Then he took the banner and returned it to the count. And just at that time, that wise man Bohemond arrived, and he gave him his own banner. The emir accepted it with great joy and made a pact with lord Bohemond that those pagans who wished to become Christians would remain with him, while the others he would allow to leave safe and sound and without harm. He agreed to all the demands of the emir, and then quickly placed his men inside the citadel. Not many days afterward, the emir was baptized along with all those who wished to accept Christ. Indeed, those that wished to adhere to their faith, the lord Bohemond had them led into the land of the Saracens.

This battle happened on the fourth day before the calends of July, the vigil of the apostles Peter and Paul,[80] in the reign of Lord Jesus Christ, to whom be honor and glory forever. Amen.

Here ends the ninth book. Here begins the tenth book.

The Tenth Narrative

July 1098 to August 1099

THE ATTACK ON JERUSALEM
DELAYED—AROUND JULY 3, 1098

$\mathcal{N}$ow when all our enemies were defeated in all ways possible—and for this we faithfully gave thanks to God the Three in One—they began to run away here and there. Some were half alive, others wounded, and they fell and died in the valleys and the woods, in the plains and on the roads. And the people of Christ, namely the victorious pilgrims, returned to the city rejoicing, happy in their triumph, after defeating the enemy.

And right away, our chief leaders, that is, Godfrey, Raymond, the count of Saint-Gilles, Bohemond, the count of Normandy, Lord Robert, and the count of Flanders, and all others, sent the most noble count, Hugh Magnus, to the emperor in Constantinople, to ask him to come and take possession of the city and carry out the terms of the agreement that he had made with them. He left, but he never returned.[1]

Now, when all these things were done, our leaders gathered together to take counsel to determine which ways would be best to lead and guide the people that they might complete their journey to the Holy Sepulcher, for which they had already overcome so many hardships. It was decided in council that they would not yet enter into the land of the pagans, because in the summer it was very arid and waterless. And they fixed the length of this wait up to the calends of November.[2]

And then the leaders dispersed, and each one left for his own lands, until the end of this waiting period. And the princes had it proclaimed in all the cities that if anyone found himself in great need and lacked gold or silver, he could make an agreement to serve them, if they wanted, and they would happily take him on.[3]

RAYMOND PILET'S ADVENTURE—AROUND JULY 3, 1098

Now, there was a certain warrior in the army of the count of Saint-Gilles, whose name was Raymond Pilet.[4] He took into his service many men, warriors and foot soldiers. He went out with his collected army and bravely entered the land of the Saracens. After he went past two cities, he came to a castle which is called Talamannia.[5] The inhabitants of this castle, namely Syrians, surrendered to him right away. When they had all stayed there for eight days, messengers came to them, saying, "There is a Saracen castle very close to us, which is filled with all kinds of provisions." And so the warriors and pilgrims of Christ went to this castle at once, besieged it on all sides, and soon captured it with the help of Christ. They rounded up all the farmers of that place, and those that would not accept Christianity they killed, and let live those who chose to accept Christ.

DEFEAT AT MARRA—JULY 27, 1098

After doing this, our Franks returned joyfully to the first castle. On the third day, they went out again and came to the city of Marra,[6] which for them was nearby, and in which many Turks and Saracens had gathered from Aleppo and from all the cities and castles that were in the area. And then the barbarians came out to fight against them, and our men, determined to take them on in battle, put them to flight. But they recovered and attacked our men for the rest of the day. And their attacks lasted until the evening. Now the heat was unbearable; our men could not bear such great thirst, since they could find no water to drink. And so they wanted to return to their castle safely. But because of their sins, the Syrians and the poor ordinary pilgrims were quickly seized by fear and began to rush back. When the Turks saw them retreating, they at once began pursuing them, and victory gave them greater courage, and so many of our men gave their souls up to God, in whose love they had gathered together. This massacre happened on the fifth day of the month of July.[7] The rest of the Franks retreated into the castle,[8] and Raymond[9] stayed there with his men for several days.

DEATH OF THE BISHOP OF PUY— AUGUST 1, 1098

The others, who had remained in Antioch, lived in joy and great happiness. Their leader and shepherd was the bishop of Puy, who fell gravely ill, by God's command, and by God's will, left this age, and resting in peace, went to sleep in the Lord on the holy day which is known as Saint Peter-in-Chains.[10] And there was much sorrow and immense grief and pain in the entire army of Christ, because he was the support of the poor and the counselor of the rich. He kept the clergy in order, he preached, and he addressed the warriors, saying, "Not one among you will be saved if he does not honor the poor and look after them. Without them, you cannot be saved. Without you, they cannot live. In their daily supplications, they should be praying to God for your sins which are hurtful every day and in many ways. And so I beg you, for the love of God, be good to them and look after them as much as you can."

THE CONQUEST OF
ALBARA—AROUND SEPTEMBER 25, 1098

Not a long time afterward, that honorable man, Raymond, count of Saint-Gilles, came and went into the land of the Saracens and came upon a city which was called Albara,[11] and which he attacked with his army, captured it quickly, and killed all the Saracen men and women, great and small, that he found in there. When he took control of it and returned it to the faith of Christ, he took counsel with the wisest of his men as to how best he could, with the greatest devotion, get a bishop for this city, who would dutifully bring it back into the faith and worship of Christ, and who would take the temple of the devil[12] and consecrate it as the house of the living and true God and an oratory of the saints. Finally, they chose a wise and honorable man and took him to Antioch to be consecrated.[13] And this was done. The rest remained in Antioch, where they lived pleasantly and happily.

A DISPUTE AMONG THE LEADERS—NOVEMBER 1, 1098

When the end of the waiting period came, namely the feast of All Saints,[14] all our leaders altogether came back to Antioch and began to ask how they could make the journey to the Holy Sepulcher, saying, "The end of the waiting period is here, and it is not the time to be arguing."[15]

Now Bohemond had been asking every day about the agreement that all the chief lords had made with him about giving him the city. But the count of Saint-Gilles did not want to soften to any agreement with Bohemond, because he was afraid to perjure himself against the emperor. And so many meetings were held in the church of Saint Peter in order to do what was just. Bohemond recited his agreement and showed his costs.[16] And the count of Saint-Gilles also disclosed the words and the oath which he had made with the emperor on the counsel of Bohemond. The bishops and Duke Godfrey, the count of Flanders and the count of Normandy, and the other chief lords went apart from the rest and went to where the chair of Saint Peter is, so that they might come up with a judgment between the two. But then afterward, fearing that the path to the Holy Sepulcher might become jeopardized, they would not say what their judgment was. Then the count of Saint-Gilles said, "Before the way to the Holy Sepulcher is abandoned, if Bohemond agrees to come with us, all that has been judged by our peers, namely Duke Godfrey and the count of Flanders and Robert the Norman, and all the other chief lords, I faithfully agree to, except that which concerns my faithfulness to the emperor."[17]

Bohemond agreed to everything, and both of them promised, with their hands in the hands of the bishops, that the route to the Holy Sepulcher would not be disrupted by either of them in any way. Then Bohemond took counsel with his men in order to supply the castle at the top of the mountain with men and rations. In the same way, the count of Saint-Gilles took counsel with his own men as to how to garrison the palace of the emir Cassian as well as the tower which is over the gate of the bridge, the port of Saint Symeon—to garrison both, that is to say, with men and rations so that it might not be lacking anything for a long time.

A DESCRIPTION OF THE CITY OF ANTIOCH

This city, namely Antioch, is really beautiful and grand, because inside its walls are four enormous and very high mountains.[18] And on the highest one is built a castle, wonderful and strong.[19] Below lies the city, magnificent and well laid out, and adorned beautifully everywhere, because in it are built many churches, some three hundred, along with sixty monasteries. The patriarch[20] holds sway over a hundred and fifty-three bishops.

All around the city are two walls, the larger of which is very high and marvelously broad, and magnificently built of stones, in which are built four hundred and fifty towers.[21] The city is beautiful all over. On the east, it is hemmed in by four great mountains. On the west, by the city walls, flows a river which is called Farfar.[22] This city holds great authority, because it was founded by seventy-five kings,[23] the first among them being King Antiochus, after whom it is called Antiochia.[24] The Franks held this city under siege for eight months and one day; and then they themselves were besieged for seven weeks by the Turks and other pagans whose number was so great that never before have so many men gathered together, either Christian or pagan. Nevertheless, by the help of God and the Holy Sepulcher, they were defeated by the Christians, and then we took our ease with great gladness and happiness for five months and eight days.

THE COUNT OF SAINT-GILLES WINS MORE CITIES—NOVEMBER 23 TO DECEMBER 12, 1098

When all this ended, in the month of November, Raymond count of Saint-Gilles left Antioch with his army and came to a city called Rugia[25] and then to another which is called Albara.[26] Four days before the end of November, he came to the city of Marra,[27] in which a great multitude of Saracens and Turks and Arabs and other pagans had gathered together. The count attacked it the next morning. Not long afterward, Bohemond, along with his army, followed the counts[28] and joined up with them on the day of the Lord. And on the Monday, they bravely attacked the city from all sides with such ferocity and such courage that they were able to put up scaling ladders against the wall. But so great was the strength of the pagans that on that day nothing could strike them or harm them.

When our chief lords saw that they really could do nothing and that they labored in vain, Raymond count of Saint-Gilles got a siege tower, strong and high, built out of wood. This siege tower was laid out and built on four wheels. On the very top stood many warriors, along with Evrard the Hunter,[29] who loudly blew his horn. Below were armed warriors who pushed the siege tower close to the wall, up against one tower. When the pagans saw this, they at once made a weapon that hurled huge stones at the siege tower, so that nearly all of our warriors were killed. They also threw out Greek fire at the siege tower, hoping to burn it and destroy it.[30] But Almighty God would not let the siege tower be burned this time around—and it stood high above all the walls of the city.

And then our warriors, who were at the very top platform, namely William of Montpellier and many others, threw down immense rocks on those below who stood on the city wall and struck them on their shields, so that both shield and enemy fell back into the city and were there killed. While they were doing this, others held spears, graced with pennants, and lances, as well as hooks of iron with which to drag the enemy toward them. And so they fought on until the evening. Behind the siege tower stood the priests and the clerks in their sacred vestments, praying and begging God to defend His people and to exalt the Christians and cast down the pagans.

On the other side, our warriors fought daily with them, setting up scaling ladders against the city wall, but the courage of the pagans was so great that our men could make no headway. Nevertheless, Golfier of Daturre[31] was the first to go up the scaling ladder on the wall. But the ladder quickly broke because so many got on it. However, he got to the top of the wall, along with some others. Meanwhile, the rest got hold of another ladder, which they quickly put up against the wall, and many warriors and foot soldiers hurriedly climbed up. But the Saracens attacked them so very fiercely, on the wall and on the ground, shooting them with arrows and thrusting them through with their lances, that many of our men were afraid and leaped off the wall.

Now, while those most courageous men who remained on the wall were resisting their attacks, others, who were below the siege tower, were digging beneath the city wall. When the Saracens saw our men digging beneath the wall, at once they were afraid and ran away into the city. All this happened on a Saturday, at the hour of vespers, when the sun was setting, the eleventh day of December.

Then, through an interpreter, Bohemond told the Saracen leaders that they, along with their wives and children and their belongings, could seek refuge in a palace that is located near the gate[32] and that he would save them from death.

Then our men entered the city, and whatever goods they found in homes and in underground cellars they took as their own. When it was day, they killed all those that they found anywhere, whether man or woman. No corner of the city was free of Saracen cadavers, and one could not walk about in the streets of the city without stepping upon Saracen corpses. And Bohemond took those that he had ordered into the palace, and he took away all that they had, namely gold, silver, and other ornaments; some he had killed, and others he had sent to Antioch to be sold. The Franks stayed on in that city for one month and four days. And this was when the bishop of Orange died.[33]

THE FAMINE LEADS TO CANNIBALISM—DECEMBER 12, 1098 TO JANUARY 13, 1099

Now there were among our men those who did not find what they needed, either because of the long halt or because they were driven by hunger, for outside the city they could find nothing to seize, and so they tore apart the bodies of the dead since one could discover bezants in their stomachs. But others, in fact, cut their flesh as morsels which they cooked and ate.[34]

THE DISPUTE CONTINUES—JANUARY 4, 1099

Indeed, Bohemond could not come to an agreement with the count of Saint-Gilles about what he had asked for, and so he went back to Antioch. Therefore, without delay, Count Raymond, by way of his messengers to Antioch, summoned Duke Godfrey, the count of Flanders, Robert the Norman, and Bohemond to come to the city of Rugia, to speak with him. And so all the chief lords came and took counsel as to how they might honorably stay on the road toward the Holy Sepulcher, for which they had set out and for which they had come so far. But they could not reconcile Bohemond with Raymond, unless Raymond gave up Antioch to him. The count would not agree to this because of the oath he had given to the emperor.[35] And so the count and the duke went back to Antioch, along with Bohemond; while Count Raymond went back to Marra, where the pilgrims were. He commanded his warriors to put in order both the palace and the castle which is above the gate of the bridge of the city.

THE COUNT OF SAINT-GILLES HEADS
OUT TO JERUSALEM ON HIS OWN—JANUARY 13, 1099

When Raymond saw that no chief lord, because of him, wanted to set out on the road to the Holy Sepulcher, he set out from Marra barefoot,[36] on the thirteenth day of January, and came to Capharda,[37] where he remained for three days. And there the count of Normandy joined Count Raymond. Now the king of Caesarea[38] sent out a lot of messengers, to Marra and to Capharda, to inform the count that he wished to be at peace with him, that he would pay him a reward, that he would care for the Christian pilgrims, and give them his oath that within the bounds of his territory, they would receive no offense, and that he would give them his assurance to gladly give them horses and food for their bodies.[39]

THE CAPTURE OF CAESAREA—JANUARY 17, 1099

And so our men headed out and came and set up camp near Caesarea, by the river Farfar.[40] When the king of Caesarea saw the pavilions of the

Franks set up so close to the city, he was afraid in his heart and ordered that all supplies be withheld from them unless they moved beyond the confines of the city. And when the day broke, he sent two Turks, that is, messengers, to go with them and show them the ford of the river and then to guide them to where they could have some good plunder. And so they came to a certain valley below a castle,[41] and there they raided more than five thousand animals and enough grain and other goods, which gave the Christian army a lot to eat. Then the castle surrendered to the count and gave him horses and refined gold, and they swore upon their law[42] that they would not let any harm come to the pilgrims. We remained there for five days, and when we left we gladly came and set up our camp near a castle of the Arabs.[43] The lord of the castle, therefore, came out and made a peace agreement with the count.[44]

THE TAKING OF MANY CITIES—JANUARY TO FEBRUARY 1099

When we headed out, we came to a really beautiful city all filled with good supplies, located in a valley, and named Kephalia.[45] When its inhabitants heard that the Franks were coming, they deserted the city, as well as their gardens filled with vegetables and their homes filled with food for the body, and fled. After three days, we left that city and crossed over a high and immense mountain,[46] and we entered the valley of Desem,[47] in which was found a great abundance of all good things, and we stayed there for fifteen days.

Close to us, there was a certain castle in which had gathered a great multitude of pagans.[48] When the castle was attacked, our men would have courageously taken it, if the Saracens had not driven out a huge herd of animals. And so our men returned to their tents laden with all good things. Then, at dawn, our men took down their pavilions and set out to besiege the castle and to set up their tents around it. But the pagan men had all fled, leaving the castle empty. Our men went inside and found in all abundance grain, wine, flour, oil, and everything else that they needed. And there we devoutly celebrated the feast of the Purification of Saint Mary.[49] And there came to us messengers from the city of Camela,[50] whose king sent to the count horses and gold and made a pact with him that Christians would not be harmed in any way, but that they would be loved and honored. The king of Tripoli[51] also sent the count a message in order to make a faithful pact with him and to have friendship, if he agreed, and to send him ten horses and four mules and gold. But the count would not make any pact with him unless he agreed to become a Christian.

Finally, we left that wonderful valley and we came to a certain castle which is called Archa,[52] on a Monday, namely the second feast day, in the middle of February; and around it we pitched our tents. It was filled with innumerable pagan people, namely Turks, Saracens, Arabs, and Paulicians. They had admirably fortified the castle and defended themselves bravely. Then fourteen of our warriors went out and headed off toward the city of Tripoli, which was close to us.[53] These fourteen found about sixty Turks and some others, who had rounded up in front of them more than fifteen hundred men and animals. Strengthened by the sign of the Cross, they attacked them and were victorious, killing six of them and capturing six horses.

FURTHER ADVENTURES OF
RAYMOND PILET—FEBRUARY 16–17, 1099

Then Raymond Pilet and Raymond viscount of Tentoria[54] left the army of count Raymond[55] and came to the city of Tortosa,[56] and they bravely attacked it. It was fortified by a multitude of pagans. Finally, when evening came, they pulled back into a corner and set up camp, lighting a lot of fires, as if the entire host were there.[57] The pagans, gripped by fright, secretly ran away during the night, abandoning the city, which was filled with all kinds of goods. It also had an excellent harbor right by the sea. When morning came, our men got ready to attack, but they found it empty. And they went inside and set up their quarters until the siege of Archa. As well, nearby there is another city which is called Maraclea,[58] the emir of which made a treaty with our men, and he let our men enter the city with their banners.

MORE CITIES ARE CAPTURED—FEBRUARY TO MAY 1099

Now, Duke Godfrey and Bohemond and the count of Flanders came to the city of Lichia.[59] Bohemond separated from them and returned to Antioch. The rest went and besieged a certain city which is named Gibellus.[60] Now, when Raymond count of Saint-Gilles heard that innumerable pagan men were rushing headlong toward us for sure battle, he took counsel with his men and sent for the chief lords that were besieging Gibellus to come to his aid. When they heard this, they at once made a pact with the emir,[61] making peace with him and accepting horses and gold, and they then left the city and came to our aid. But the pagans did not come to fight us, and therefore the counts set up camp beyond the river[62] and also took up the siege.

Not long afterward, our men rode out against Tripoli, and outside the city they found Turks, Arabs, and Saracens, whom our men attacked and put to flight, killing a great many of the nobles of the city. So many pagans were killed and so much blood spilled that the water which flowed into the city appeared red when it flowed into their cisterns, and this made them sad and sorrowful, and indeed they were so afraid that none of them dared to go outside the city gate.

Another day, our men rode out to Desem and found oxen and sheep and donkeys and many other animals, and they also made off with nearly three thousand camels. We besieged the castle already mentioned for three months less a day, and while there we celebrated Easter four days before the Ides of April.[63] Now, our ships came up close to us into a certain port,[64] during the time when the siege was still going on, and they brought us a lot of supplies, namely grain, wine, and meat and cheese and barley and oil, so that the entire expedition had a lot of provisions. And during that same siege, many of our men received blessed martyrdom, namely Anselm of Ribemont,[65] William the Picard,[66] and so many others whom I do not know.

Now, the king of Tripoli[67] often sent messengers to the chief lords to leave the castle and make a peace treaty with him. When our men heard this, namely Duke Godfrey and Raymond count of Saint-Gilles and Robert the Norman and the count of Flanders, and they saw that the new harvest was beginning, since by the middle of March we were eating new beans, and by the middle of April we had wheat, our men took counsel and decided that it would be good to complete the journey to Jerusalem as the new harvest was coming in.

Therefore we left the castle and came to Tripoli on the sixth feast day, the thirteenth day of May, and we remained there for three days. In the end, the king of Tripoli made a treaty with the chief lords and at once handed over to them more than three hundred pilgrims that he had captured, and he also gave to them fifteen thousand bezants and fifteen horses of great value. He also gave us lots of supplies: horses, donkeys, and all kinds of goods, which enriched all of the army of Christ. He also agreed with the chief lords that if they won the war they were preparing against the emir of Babylon and they took Jerusalem, he would become Christian and hold his land from them. And so it was done and agreed upon.

On the second feast day, in the month of May,[68] we left that city and for the whole day and night followed a path that was both narrow and steep. And we came to a castle named Bethelon,[69] near a city by the sea that was called Zebar,[70] where we suffered terribly from thirst, and so we were exhausted when we came to the river named Braym.[71] Then on the day of the Ascension of our Lord,[72] for the whole day and night, we crossed a mountain by a path that was very narrow. And we thought that we would find our enemies waiting in ambush, but by the will of God none of them dared to come before us. Then our warriors went in front of us, freeing up the path for us. And so we reached a city beside the sea, which is called Baruth.[73] From there, we came to another city which is called Sagitta,[74] and then to another which is called Sur,[75] and from Sur to the city of Acre.[76] From Acre we came to a castle which is named Cayphas,[77] and soon we were encamped next to Caesarea, where we celebrated Pentecost, the third day before the end of May.

Then we came to the city of Ramola,[78] which the Saracens had abandoned for fear of the Franks, and close to which is the venerable church in which rests the precious body of Saint George who, for the name of Christ, suffered blessed martyrdom there at the hands of the pagans.[79] And our leaders decided in council to elect a bishop who would take care of this church and govern it, and they gave him tithes and gold and silver as well as horses and other animals that he might live devoutly and honorably with those that were with him. And he remained there gladly.[80]

ARRIVAL AT JERUSALEM—JUNE 7, 1099

And then, joyfully and cheerfully, we came to the city of Jerusalem, on the third feast day, eight days before the Ides of June.[81] And there we set up a marvelous siege. Now, Robert the Norman laid his siege on the north side, near the church of Saint Stephen, the first martyr, who was stoned there for the name of Christ.[82] Robert the count of Flanders was next to him. To the west, Duke Godfrey and Tancred laid their siege. The count of Saint-Gilles set up his siege in the middle, namely on Mount Zion, around the church of Saint Mary, the mother of the Lord, and where the Lord had the Last Supper with His disciples.[83]

THE SIEGE OF JERUSALEM—JUNE 7 TO JULY 8, 1099

Now, on the third day, some of our men, that is, Raymond Pilet and Raymond of Taurina,[84] and many others, separated from the army and headed off to fight, and they attacked about a hundred Arabs, and the warriors of Christ fought against those unbelievers. By the help of God, they bravely defeated them and killed many of them; and they also captured thirty horses.

On the following second feast day,[85] we attacked the city so bravely and so marvelously that had we prepared our scaling ladders, the city would have been in our hands. We destroyed the outer wall and put up a ladder against the main wall, and our warriors went up it and fought the Saracens and defenders of the city at close quarters with their swords and lances. Many of our men, but more of theirs, met their death. But during this siege we were not able to find bread to buy for a period of ten days, until a messenger arrived from our ships. As well, we were suffering terribly from thirst, and we had to take our horses and other animals six miles to water them, despite many terrors. Though the pool of Siloam sustained us, still water was sold very expensively among us.[86]

After the messenger came from our ships,[87] our chief lords took counsel among themselves as to how they might send warriors who would faithfully guard both men and ships in the port of Japha.[88] At dawn, a hundred warriors set off from Raymond count of Saint-Gilles's army, namely Raymond Pilet, Achard of Montmerle,[89] and William of Sabran,[90] and boldly they headed off for the port. Then thirty of our warriors separated from the others and came upon seven hundred Arabs and Turks and Saracens from the army of the emir. The warriors of

Christ bravely attacked them. But so great was the courage of the others that they overcame our men and surrounded them, and they killed Achard of Montmerle and some poor men on foot.

When our men were thus hemmed in, and all of them expecting death, a messenger came up to Raymond Pilet and said, "What are you doing here with these warriors? Behold, all our men are struggling badly with Arabs and Turks and Saracens, and maybe at this very hour they have all been put to death. Therefore, rescue them, rescue them!"

Hearing this, our men quickly rode by the fastest way and rapidly came to where they were fighting. The pagan men, seeing the warriors of Christ, divided themselves and formed two battalions. But our men, invoking the name of Christ, attacked these unbelievers so ferociously that each warrior struck down his adversary. And when they saw that they could not withstand the courage of the Franks, and struck by deep terror, they turned their backs. Our men pursued them for a space of some four miles, killing many of them. And they left one alive from whom they could find out details. Also, they captured one hundred and three horses.

During the siege, so oppressed were we by thirst that we sewed the skin of oxen and buffaloes in which we carried water for a space of six miles. Indeed, out of such stinking vessels we drank water, and because of such reeking water and barley bread, we suffered and were tormented daily. And the Saracens secretly lay hidden by each fountain and spring and there they killed our men and then cut them into pieces. Also, they led off our animals into their caverns and their caves.

Then our chief lords looked into how the city could be taken by siege engines, so that we might worship inside the Sepulcher of our Savior. They made two wooden siege towers and many other besieging machines. Duke Godfrey set up a siege tower that had besieging machines, and count Raymond did likewise, although they had to bring the timber from very far away. When the Saracens saw our men making these machines, they marvelously fortified the city and strengthened the towers during the night.

Then our chief lords saw which part of the city was the weakest, and during one Saturday night,[91] they transported our machine and wooden siege tower to the eastern sector. They put the engines in place at dawn, and then they set up and fortified the siege tower on the first, second, and third feast days. The count of Saint-Gilles set up his machine in the southern sector. And all this time, so terribly were we suffering from thirst that a man could not buy enough water even for a denier to quench his thirst.

THE ATTACK ON JERUSALEM—JULY 13–14, 1099

On the fourth and fifth feast day,[92] we launched a marvelous attack on the city, both during the day and at night. But before we could attack, the bishops and the priests ordered us, by all the sermons and exhortations, to do a procession, in God's honor, around Jerusalem, praying and celebrating and then faithfully giving alms and fasting.

On the sixth feast day,[93] at daybreak, we attacked the city from all sides, but we could do it no harm. And we were all bewildered and also quite afraid. Then, when that hour approached when our Lord Jesus Christ had consented to suffer by being put on the Cross, our warriors fought valiantly upon the siege tower, namely Duke Godfrey and Count Eustace his brother.[94] Then a certain warrior from among us, named Lethold,[95] got on top of the city wall. And as soon as he got on top, all the defenders of the city fled from the walls and into the city, and our men followed and chased after them, killing and cutting them down right up to the Temple of Solomon,[96] where there was so much slaughter that our men put down their feet in blood up to the ankle.

Now, Count Raymond, from the southern sector, was leading his army and siege tower up near the wall. But between the siege tower and the wall was a ditch. And so it was proclaimed that whoever brought three stones to the ditch would be given a denier. It took three days and nights to fill the pit; once it was filled, the siege tower was brought up close to the wall; those who were inside fought marvelously against us with fire and rocks. When the count heard that the Franks were in the city, he said to his men, "Why are you slow? Behold, all the Franks are already in the city."

JERUSALEM IS CONQUERED—JULY 15, 1099

Then the emir[97] who was in the Tower of David[98] surrendered to the count and he opened that gate where the pilgrims used to pay their tributes. Inside the city, our pilgrims chased after and killed Saracens right up to the Temple of Solomon,[99] where they had gathered and where they fought furiously against our men the whole day, until their blood ran throughout the temple. When the pagans were defeated, our men captured men and women in the temple and they killed those that they wanted and they let live those that they chose. On top of the Temple of Solomon were gathered a great many pagans, of both sexes. To these Tancred and Gaston of Beert[100] gave their banners. And then our men rushed throughout the city, seizing gold and silver, horses and mules, and houses filled with all good things.

And finally, our men came rejoicing and weeping with happiness to the Sepulcher of our Savior Jesus to adore it and to render their great debt to Him. The next morning, our men climbed up on the roof of the temple and attacked the Saracens, both men and women, beheading them with naked swords. Some of them jumped from the temple. Seeing this, Tancred was filled with anger.

Then our men took counsel and decided that each one should give alms and pray that God might choose someone who pleased Him to rule over the others and to rule the city. They also ordered that all the dead Saracens be thrown outside the city because of the terrible stench, because the entire city was filled with their corpses. And the living Saracens carried the dead ones out to the front of the gate and made mounds out of them as high as houses. There were so many dead pagan men that no one has heard of nor seen the like; and they were then laid up on pyres. And as to how many there were, no one knows, except God. But Count Raymond led away the emir and those that were with him to Scalona[101] safe and sound.

DUKE GODFREY IS ELECTED THE FIRST LATIN RULER OF JERUSALEM—JULY 22, 1099

Then, on the eighth day after the city was captured, they elected Duke Godfrey as the prince of the city that he might fight the pagans and guard the Christians. Likewise, on the day of Saint Peter in Chains,[102] they elected as patriarch a most wise and honorable man named Arnulf.[103] This city was captured by God's Christians on the fifteenth day of July, on the sixth feast day.[104]

NABLUS SURRENDERS—JULY 25 TO AUGUST 4, 1099

Meanwhile, a messenger came to Tancred and to Count Eustace inviting them to prepare to receive the city of Neopolitana.[105] And they set out and took with them many warriors and foot soldiers and came to that city. Indeed, the inhabitants surrendered to them at once.

THE MARCH TO SCALONA—AUGUST 4–9, 1099

Then the duke[106] commanded them to come quickly to stop an attack that the emir of Babylon[107] was preparing against the city of Scalona. And so they hurried into the mountains looking for Saracens to fight, and then they came to Caesarea. Then they followed the sea up to the city of Ramola, where they found many Arabs who were lookouts for the battalion. Our men chased them and captured many of them, who gave all the details of the battle: where they were, and how many, and where they were planning to engage in battle with the Christians. Hearing this, Tancred at once sent a messenger to Jerusalem, to Duke Godfrey, to the patriarch and to all the other princes, saying, "You should know that a battle is being prepared against us at Scalona. Therefore, come quickly with all the strength that you have available."

Then the duke commanded that everyone be summoned so that they might faithfully get ready to go to Scalona against our enemies. And he, along with the patriarch and Robert count of Flanders left the city on the third feast day;[108] and with them went the bishop of Martura.[109]

Now, the count of Saint-Gilles and Robert the Norman said that they would not go out unless they knew that a battle was certain. Therefore, they commanded their warriors to go on ahead and see if there indeed was about to be a battle, and to come back very quickly, because they were ready to head out. So, they went out and saw that a battle was being prepared, and they hurried back and told them what they had seen with their own eyes. The duke at once got hold of the bishop of Martura and sent him to Jerusalem to order the warriors there to get ready and come to fight.

On the fourth feast day,[110] these princes left and marched off to battle. Now the bishop of Martura was returning and bringing back the words of the messages to the patriarch and the duke, when the Saracens moved against him and captured him and took him with them.

Now, Peter the Hermit had remained in Jerusalem to make arrangements and to command Greek and Latin priests to celebrate a procession in honor of God, and to offer prayers and alms that God may give victory to His people. The priests and the presbyters, wearing their sacred vestments, led a procession to the temple of the Lord,[111] and they sang masses and orations that He might defend His people.

Finally, the patriarch and the bishops and the chief lords gathered at the river[112] which is at the side of Scalona. They raided many animals there, oxen, camels, sheep, and many other good things. Then about three hundred Arabs arrived, and our men went at them, capturing two and driving the rest back to their army. When evening came, the patriarch made it known throughout the host[113] that in the morning everyone was to prepare for battle, while excommunicating any man who intended to look for plunder before the battle was over; however, after the battle, they could gladly go back and take whatever the Lord had already determined for them.

THE ATTACK ON SCALONA—AUGUST 9, 1099

Then, at dawn, they went into a beautiful valley, by the seashore,[114] where they drew up their battle formations. The Duke put his formation into order, as did the count of Normandy, the count of Saint-Gilles, the count of Flanders, Count Eustace, Tancred, and Gaston.[115] They commanded that the foot soldiers and the archers should go in front of the warriors. And all this was quickly done, and they went into battle, in the name of Lord Jesus Christ.

On the left side was Duke Godfrey with his formation, and the count of Saint-Gilles rode next to the sea on the right side. The count of Normandy and the count of Flanders and Tancred and all the others rode in the middle. In this way, our men began to slowly move forward. The pagans also stood ready for battle. And each one of them had a vessel hanging from his neck, from which to drink as he pursued us. But by the grace of God, this was not to be.

The count of Normandy, having picked out the standard of the emir which had a golden apple on top that was covered in silver, rushed fiercely at the man who carried it and mortally wounded him. On the other side, the count of Flanders ardently attacked them. And Tancred, from the middle, made an assault on their tents. When the pagans saw all this, they took to flight. How vast and innumerable was their multitude, none knows, except God. The battle was ferocious, but a divine force was with us, which was so great, so powerful that we defeated them at once.

Indeed, the enemies of God were blinded and stupefied, for though they looked upon the warriors of Christ with open eyes, they did not see them, and they did not dare stand up against the Christians, for the power of God terrified them. And in their terror, they climbed up into trees where they might hide, but our men killed them with arrows, lances, and swords so that they fell to the earth. Still others threw themselves to the ground, not daring to stand up against us. And so our men beheaded them just like you would behead an animal in the market. Next to the sea, the count of Saint-Gilles slaughtered them without number; some leaped into the sea, while others fled here and there.

Then the emir came up before the city, grieving and sorrowing, and he said, weeping, "O spirits of the gods. Who has seen or heard of such things? Such might, such courage, such an army has never before been defeated by any nation, as has been defeated by these few Christian people. Alas, what pain and suffering for me. What more can I say? I have been defeated by a race of beggars, unarmed and poverty stricken, who have nothing but a sack and a beggar's bag. And they are the ones now pursuing the Egyptian people who used to distribute alms to them when they roamed about, begging all over our homeland.[116] I enlisted and brought here two hundred thousand warriors, and I now see them fleeing with slackened reins along the road to Babylon, and they do not want to turn back and face the Frankish people. I swear by Mohamed and by the splendor of all the gods that never again will I undertake to raise an army because I have been driven off by such a strange people. I brought all kinds of weapons and war machines to besiege them in Jerusalem, and it is they who attacked me two days earlier. Alas! What more can I say? I shall always be dishonored in the land of Babylon."[117]

Our men took his standard, which the count of Normandy then bought for twenty silver marks[118] and gave to the patriarch in honor of

God and of the Holy Sepulcher. And his sword was bought by someone for sixty bezants.

And in this way were our enemies defeated, by the will of God. All the ships of the pagan lands were there. But when the men who were in them saw the emir fleeing with his army, they quickly hoisted sail and headed for the high seas.

Our men went back to the enemy's tents and gathered up a lot of plunder, gold, silver, and heaps of other good things, as well as animals of all kinds, and all kinds of weapons and utensils. They took away what they could and let fire burn the rest.

THE RETURN TO JERUSALEM—AUGUST 13, 1099

Then our men returned to Jerusalem, carrying with them all the goods that they needed. This battle was fought on the day before the Ides of August,[119] by the grace of our Lord Jesus Christ, to whom be honor and glory now and forever, from age to age. Let every soul say, "Amen!"

Description of the Holy Places of Jerusalem

$\mathscr{I}$f he who wants to visit Jerusalem from the western areas, let him always hold to the rising sun, and he will discover Jerusalem's places of prayer, which are noted here.

In Jerusalem, there is a little room, which has a single stone for a roof, where Solomon wrote the Book of Wisdom.[1] And there, between the temple and the altar, upon the marble before the sanctuary, the blood of Zechariah was spilled.[2]

From there, not far away is a stone to which Jews come every year and which they anoint, lamenting, and then go away groaning.[3]

There is the house of Hezekiah, the king of Judah, to whom God gave three times five years.[4]

Next is the house of Caiaphas, and the column to which Christ was bound and struck with a whip.

At the Neapolitana Gate, is Pilate's Pretorium, where Jesus was judged by the high priests.

And there, not far off, is Golgotha, that is, the place of the skull, where Christ the Son of God was crucified, and where the first Adam was buried, and where Abraham sacrificed to God.

From there, a great stone's throw toward the west, is located the spot where Joseph of Arimathea buried the holy body of Lord Jesus Christ; and there is the splendid church built by King Constantine.[5]

On Mount Calvary, toward the west, are the thirteen feet to the center of the world. On the left side is the prison where Christ was imprisoned. On the right side, by the Sepulcher, is the Latin monastery in honor of the Holy Virgin Mary, where her house was. In that monastery is an altar where Mary the Virgin Mother stood, and with her, Mary of Cleopas, the sister of her mother, and Mary Magdalene, crying and grieving when they saw the Lord hanging on the cross. It was there that Jesus said to his mother, "Woman, behold thy son," and to the disciple, "Behold thy mother."[6]

From this location, some two bowshots away, in the eastern side, is the Temple of the Lord, which Solomon built, in which Christ was presented by the righteous Simeon.[7] To the right side of this temple, Solomon built his own temple, and on both sides of the temple, he built a splendid portico of marble columns. On the left side is the Pool of Testing.[8]

From there, toward the east, about a thousand paces, the Mount of Olives can be seen, where the Lord prayed to the Father, saying, "Father, if it be possible," and so on.[9] And upon a stone, He wrote the "Our Father." And from there, He ascended into Heaven, saying to his disciples, "Go, and teach all nations," and so on.[10]

Between the Temple of the Lord and the Mount of Olives is the Valley of Jehoshaphat, where the Virgin Mary was buried by the Apostles. In this valley the Lord will come to judge the world.

Close to there is the village which is called Gethsemane, and close to that is the garden, across the brook of Cedron, where Judas betrayed Jesus.

From there, and close by, is the tomb of Isaiah the prophet.

From there, about a thousand paces, is Bethany, where Lazarus, on the fourth day, was revived.

In that same area, nineteen miles out toward Jericho, is the sycamore tree that Zachaeus climbed to see Jesus.

On the other side, a thousand paces from Jericho, is the spring of Elisha, which he himself blessed by stirring in salt.

From there, five miles out, is the Jordan River, in which the Lord was baptized by John. It is eight leagues in distance from Jerusalem.

Not far away from there is the mountain from which Elijah was carried away into Heaven.

From the Jordan, the road is eighteen days out toward Mount

Sinai, where God appeared to Moses in the burning bush and where He gave the Law; and there sits a great jar, which never ceases to produce oil.

Mount Tabor is a three-day journey from Jerusalem, where the Lord was transfigured. It is said that at the foot of this mountain are Galilee and the Sea of Tiberias, which is not a sea but a lake, from which the Jordan flows out.

On the right side of the city of Jerusalem, south of the wall, about a bowshot out, is Mount Zion, and over there is a church built by Solomon. There Jesus had the Last Supper with the disciples before the Passion; and there He filled them with the Holy Ghost. And there, the Virgin Mary left the world and gave up her spirit, whose body the holy Apostles then carried over to the Valley of Jehoshaphat.

At the foot of this mountain, to the south, is the Pool of Siloam, which gushes quickly out of the earth.

From there, and not far away, is Sychem, where Joseph came from the valley of Hebron, seeking his brothers. There is the village which Jacob gave to his son Joseph. And there his body rests.

From there, a thousand paces, is Sychar, where the Lord spoke with the Samaritan woman.

From there, not far, is the place where the angel wrestled with Jacob. And there is Bethlehem, the city of David, where Christ was born, a distance of four miles to the south. And a church of marble is built, with marble columns, there where Christ was born. Not far off from there is the Lord's manger.

From there, twelve miles on, is the castle of Abraham, which is called Tocor, where Abraham himself and Isaac and Jacob are buried, along with their wives.

To the left is the mountain "the Lord sees," which is where Abraham wanted to sacrifice his son.

Here ends the Jerusalem Itinerary.

Mass in Veneration of the Holy Sepulcher

*A*lmighty, eternal God, who, through the Passion of Thine Only-Begotten, hath allowed humankind to be redeemed, and by His burial hath marked the burial of all the faithful, we entreat Thee to grant that we may become worthy of sharing in His resurrection. Through him . . .

THE SECRETUM. Accept, we ask Thee, Almighty God, this sacrificial host, which we present Thee in the memory of Him who to cleanse the sins of the world gently suffered the cross and the grave for us, and who lives with Thee . . .

THE PREFACE. O eternal God, who, through the mouths of the prophets, made known the glory of Thine Only-Begotten, whose flesh did not see corruption in the famed Sepulcher, so that as Victor He rose from the dead, thus giving hope of resurrection to the faithful. And so with angels, etc.

POSTCOMMUNION. May the promise of our redemption, we pray, Almighty God, which we have received through faith, destroy the Sepulcher of our sins and lead us to the glory of a blessed resurrection. Through our Lord . . .

THE DIMENSIONS OF THE HOLY SEPULCHER

This line, copied from the Sepulcher of the Lord at Jerusalem, and increased by fifteen, designates the height of Christ. The day you see it, you shall die a sudden death.[1]

This second one, rendered by the number nine, signifies the width of Christ, and it too gives protection against sudden death, just as on the day when it was seen.[2]

Verse in Praise of Bohemond

Now the world resonates with the things that Bohemond did:
The deeds of Bohemond peal through the regions of the world.
May the light and glory of the world be on Bohemond:
Fame runs through the world entire, loudly shouting, "Bohemond!"[1]

Four Names

Peter, the clerk of Mirabeau. William, the clerk of Vosailles. Walter of Fontfroide, layman. John of Gélis, layman.[1]

Notes

INTRODUCTION

1. Including the *Gesta*, there are a total of twelve historical chronicles of the First Crusade. The other eleven are:

1. Albert of Aachen: *Historia Ierosolimitana*, ed. and trans. S. Edgington (Oxford: Oxford Medieval Texts, 2007).
2. Baudri of Bourgueil: *Historia Hierosolymitana*, Recueil des historiens des croisades: historiens occidentaux, Vol. 4 (Paris: l'Académie royale, 1879).
3. Ekkehard of Aura: *Ekkehardi Uruagensis Hierosolymita: De oppressione liberatione ac restautatione Jerosolymitanae Ecclesiae*, Recueil des historiens des croisades: historiens occidentaux, Vol. 5 (Paris: l'Académie royale, 1895).
4. Fulcher of Chartres: *Fulcheri Carnotensis Historia Hierosolymitana (1095–1127)*, ed. Heinrich Hagenmeyer (Heidelberg: Carl Winter, 1913).
5. Fulcher of Chartres: *Gesta Francorum Hierusalem Expugnantium*, Recueil des historiens des croisades: historiens occidentaux, Vol. 3 (Paris: l'Académie royale, 1866). An abbreviated version of Fulcher's chronicle above.
6. Guibert of Nogent: *Guibertus abbas S. Mariae Nogenti, Dei gesta per Francos*, ed. Robert B. C. Huygens, Corpus Christianorum, Continuatio Mediaevalis, 127A (Turnhout: Brepols, 1996).
7. Monte Cassino Chronicle: *Historia peregrinorum euntium Jerusolymam ad liberandum Sanctum Sepulcrum de potestate ethnicorum*, Recueil

des historiens des croisades: historiens occidentaux, Vol. 3 (Paris: l'Académie royale, 1866).

8. Peter Tudebode: *Historia de Hierosolymitano itinere*, ed. John H. Hill and Laurita L. Hill (Paris: Paul Geuthner, 1977).

9. Ralph of Caen: *Gesta Tancredi*, Recueil des historiens des croisades: historiens occidentaux, Vol. 3 (Paris: l'Académie royale, 1866).

10. Raymond d'Aguilers: *Le "Liber" de Raymond d'Aguilers*, ed. John H. Hill and Laurita L. Hill (Paris: Paul Geuthner, 1969).

11. Robert the Monk: *Roberti Monachi historia Iherosolimitana*, Recueil des historiens des croisades: historiens occidentaux, Vol. 3 (Paris: l'Académie royale, 1866).

2. See, for example, Jay Rubenstein, "What Is the *Gesta Francorum*, and Who Was Peter Tudebode?" in *Revue Mabillon* 16 (2005), pp. 179–204.

3. See Hugo Buchthal, *Miniature Painting in the Latin Kingdom of Jerusalem, with liturgical and paleographic chapters by Francis Wormald* (New York: Oxford University Press; London: Warburg Institute, 1957).

4. *Ekkehardi Uruagensis Hierosolymita: De oppressione liberatione ac restautatione Jerosolymitanae Ecclesiae*, Recueil des historiens des croisades: historiens occidentaux, Vol. 5 (Paris: l'Académie royale, 1895), p. 21.

5. Summarized in Hill. See Rosalind Hill, ed. and trans., *The Deeds of the Franks and Other Pilgrims to Jerusalem* (Oxford: Clarendon Press, 1979), pp. xi–xvi.

6. See Rubenstein (2005).

7. What Rubenstein calls a "Jerusalem History."

8. See Yuval N. Harari, "Eyewitnessing in Accounts of the First Crusade: The Gesta Francorum and Other Contemporary Narratives," in *Crusades* 3 (2004), pp. 77–99; and Elizabeth Lapina, "Nec signis nec testibus creditor. The Problem of Eyewitnesses in the Chronicles of the First Crusade," in *Viator: Medieval and Renaissance Studies* 38 (2007), pp. 117–139.

9. See note 1.

10. Throughout the Old Testament, God is often called the "Lord of hosts." The crusaders are therefore also God's army. For example, see Isaiah 47:4 (Our Redeemer, the Lord of hosts is His name, the holy one of Israel), or Isaiah 31:4b (So will the Lord of hosts come down to wage war on Mount Zion and on its hill). All quotations from the Bible throughout are from the New American Standard Bible.

11. For the context of Urban's speech, see Thomas Asbridge, *The First Crusade: A New History* (New York: Oxford University Press, 2004), pp. 32–39.

12. For a detailed examination of the effects of the Viking raids on the crumbling Carolingian world see Thomas O. Kay, *The Effect of the Viking Raids on the French Monasteries* (Chicago: The University of Chicago Press, 1974). See also Einar Joranson, *The Danegeld in France* (Rock Island: Augustana, 1923).

13. See Marc Bloch's *Feudal Society: The Growth of Ties of Dependence*, trans. L.A. Manyon (London: Routledge & Kegan Paul Ltd., 1962), pp. 275ff.

14. Bloch (1962), pp. 441ff.

15. See H.E.J. Cowdrey, "The Peace and the Truce of God in the Eleventh Century," in *Past & Present* 46(1970), pp. 42–67.

16. See Joseph P. Lynch, *Simoniacal Entry into Religious Life from 1000 to 1260: A Social, Economic, and Legal Study* (Columbus: Ohio State University Press, 1976).

17. For the life of Saint Gerald, see Thomas F.X. Noble and Thomas Head, eds., *Soldiers of Christ: Saints and Saints' Lives from Late Antiquity and the Early Middle Ages* (University Park, PA: The Pennsylvania State University Press, 1995), pp. 293ff.

18. See Barbara H. Rosenwein, *Rhinoceros Bound: Cluny in the Tenth Century* (Philadelphia: University of Pennsylvania Press, 1982).

19. Marcus Bull sees the response to the First Crusade as rooted in this relationship of obligation between the Church and the nobility. See his *Knightly Piety and the Lay Response to the First Crusade. The Limousin and Gascony, c. 970–c. 1130* (Oxford: Clarendon, 1993).

20. See the important study by Kassius Hallinger, *Gorze–Kluny: Studien zu den monastischen Lebensformen und Gegensätzen im Hochmittelalter*, 2 vols. (Rome: Herder, 1950–1951).

21. See Patrick J. Geary, *Living with the Dead in the Middle Ages* (Ithaca: Cornell University Press, 1994), pp. 177–220, and also his *Furta Sacra: The Theft of Relics in the Central Middle Ages* (Princeton, NJ: Princeton University Press, 1990).

22. See Gerd Tellenbach, *The Church in Western Europe from the Tenth to the Early Twelfth Century* (Cambridge: Cambridge University Press, 1993).

23. See Uta-Renate Blumenthal, *The Investiture Controversy. Church and Monarchy from the Ninth to the Twelfth Century* (Philadelphia: University of Pennsylvania Press, 1988).

24. Gordon S. Brown, *The Norman Conquests of Southern Italy and Sicily* (Jefferson, NC: McFarland & Company, 2003).

25. See Alexios G.C. Savvides, *Byzantino-Normannica: The Norman Capture of Italy (to A.D. 1081) and the First Two Invasions in Byzantium. A.D. 1081–1085 and 1107–1108* (Leuven: Peeters, 2007).

26. See A.C.S. Peacock, *Early Seljuq History: A New Interpretation* (New York: Routledge, 2010).

27. See Michael Angold, "The Battle of Manzikert," in *Manzikert to Lepanto: The Byzantine World and the Turks 1071–1571*, eds., Anthony Bryer and Michael Ursinus (Amsterdam: A.M. Hakkert, 1991), pp. 9–34.

28. See Claude Cahen, *The Formation of Turkey: The Seljukid Sultanate of Rum: Eleventh to the Fourteenth Century*, trans. P.M. Holt (Harlow, UK: Longman, 2001).

29. See Ferdinand Chalandon, *Essai sur le règne d'Alexis Ier Comnène. 1081–1118* (New York: B. Franklin, 1960).

30. See John W. Birkenmeier, *The Development of the Komnenian Army, 1081–1180* (Leiden; Boston: Brill, 2002).

31. See John France, *The Crusades and the Expansion of Catholic Christendom* (New York: Routledge, 2005), pp. 23ff.

32. Over the years, the churches in the East and the West had become separated over differences in rites and liturgy, leading to the establishment of a distinct Roman Catholic Church and an Eastern Orthodox Church, one Latin and the other Greek. These differences remain unresolved to this day. See Henry Chadwick, *East and West: The Making of a Rift in the Church from Apostolic Times until the Council of Florence* (Oxford/New York: Oxford University Press, 2003).

33. See Jonathan Riley-Smith, *The First Crusade and the Idea of Crusading* (London: Continuum, 2003), pp. 13–30.

34. See Jean Flori, *Pierre l'Ermite et la première croisade* (Paris: Fayard, 1999).

35. On the logistics of supplying the crusader army see Bernard S. Bachrach, "Crusader Logistics: From Victory at Nicaea to Resupply at Dorylaion," in *Logistics of Warfare in the Age of the Crusades*, ed. John Pryor (Aldershot: Ashgate, 2006), pp. 43–62; Charles Glasheen, "Provisioning Peter the Hermit: From Cologne to Constantinople, 1096," in Pryor (2006), pp. 119–129; and Alan V. Murray, "Money and Logistics in the Forces of the First Crusade: Coinage, Bullion, Service, and Supply, 1096–1099," in Pryor (2006), pp. 229–249.

36. The classic study of the Christian underpinnings of the crusades remains Paul Alphandéry, *La chrétienté et l'idée de croisade*, 2 vols. (Paris: Albin Michel, 1954–1959).

37. See Robert Chazan, *European Jewry and the First Crusade* (Berkeley and Los Angeles: University of California Press, 1987). The scale and extent of the violence might well have been exaggerated, Chazan suggests (pp. 62–63).

38. Michel Rouche, "Cannibalisme sacré chez les croisères populaires," in *Religion populaire: Aspects de christianisme populaire à travers l'histoire*, ed. Yves-Marie Hilaire (Lille: Centre interdisciplinaire d'études des religions de l'Université de Lille III, 1981), pp. 31–41.

39. See Geraldine Heng, *Empire of Magic: Medieval Romance and the Politics of Cultural Fantasy* (New York: Columbia University Press, 2003), pp. 17ff.

40. Jay Rubenstein, "Cannibals and Crusaders," in *French Historical Studies*, 31(4), 2008, pp. 525–552.

41. The extent of the slaughter at Jerusalem in 1099 has been a contentious issue among historians. It was once commonplace to present the crusaders as cold-blooded killers of everyone inside the city, with figures of their murdered victims ranging from 30,000 to 40,000 individuals. A typical representative of this view is the work of John France, *Victory in the East: A Military History of the First Crusade* (Cambridge: Cambridge University Press, 1999), pp. 355–356. A soberer, and more accurate, account is given by Benjamin Z. Kedar who reinforces the allegorical nature of the literary descriptions of the slaughter by suggesting that the number of individuals killed by the crusaders was no more than 3,000. The slaughter of civilians was a sad fact of medieval warfare in the Middle East as well as in Europe. Therefore, the massacre at Jerusalem should not be taken as an instance of European cruelty in a non-European setting, and it must be understood in the context of its time. See Kedar's comprehensive article, "The Jerusalem Massacre of July 1099 in the Western Historiography of the Crusades," *Crusades 3* (2004), 15–75.

42. Jacques Bongars, ed., *Gesta Dei per Francos* (Hanover, Aubrius, 1611). P. Le Bas, ed., *Recueil des historiens des croisades: Historiens occidentaux*, Vol. 3 (Paris: l'Académie royale, 1866), pp. 121–163. Heinrich Hagenmeyer, ed., *Anonymi Gesta Francorum et aliorum Hierosolymitanorum* (Heidelberg: C. Winter, 1890). Louis Bréhier, ed., *Histoire anonyme de la première croisade* (Paris: H. Champion, 1924). Rosalind Hill, ed. and trans., *The Deeds of the Franks and the Other Pilgrims to Jerusalem* (Oxford: Clarendon Press, 1979).

43. The most notorious of which is linking the author closely with Bohemond by adding what is missing in the original. For example, she consistently gives "my lord Bohemond," when the original simply states, "lord Bohemond."

THE FIRST NARRATIVE

1. This statement of Jesus is found in the Synoptic Gospels: "Then Jesus said to His disciples, 'If anyone wishes to come after Me, he must deny himself, and take up his cross and follow Me'" (Matthew 16:24). A similar statement is found in Mark 8:34 and Luke 9:23.

2. In the context of the eleventh century, "Gaul" was a geographical designation, since the region later to be known as France was at this time a conglomera-

tion of various principalities with very fluid borders. See Jean Dunbabin, *France in the Making, 843–1180* (Oxford: Oxford University Press, 2000), 162–222.

3. i.e., the pope, who is the bishop of Rome, and as Peter's representative, he is also designated as the Apostle of Rome in medieval sources.

4. Elected in 1088, Urban would reign as pope for eleven years. He was born in the Champagne region of France.

5. This refers to France, the land that lies beyond the Alps.

6. A denier was a silver penny current in France until the French Revolution. It contained roughly two-and-a-half grams of silver.

7. A version of Acts 9:16: "For I will show him how much he must suffer for My name's sake."

8. A combination of 2 Timothy 1:8 (Therefore do not be ashamed of the testimony of our Lord or of me His prisoner, but join with me in suffering for the gospel according to the power of God), and Luke 21:15 (For I will give you utterance and wisdom which none of your opponents will be able to resist or refute).

9. A reference to either Matthew 5:12 (Rejoice and be glad, for your reward in heaven is great; for in the same way they persecuted the prophets who were before you) or Colossians 3:24 (knowing that from the Lord you will receive the reward of the inheritance. It is the Lord Christ whom you serve).

10. i.e., Hell.

11. This phrase has a distant literary echo in Julius Caesar's famous introductory remark, "Gallia est omnis divisa in partes tres (everywhere Gaul is divided into three parts)" which begins his book on the Gallic wars. See Julius Caesar, *The Gallic War: Seven Commentaries on the Gallic War with an Eighth Commentary by Aulus Hirtius*, trans. Carolyn Hammond (Oxford: Oxford University Press, 1996), 1. As well, the author of the *Gesta* is stating the fact that the crusaders took three different routes to get to Constantinople.

12. Peter the Hermit (ca. 1050–1115) was a priest from Amiens, who popularized the idea of the First Crusade and in the spring of 1096, led a ragtag army of commoners to liberate Christ's tomb, or the Holy Sepulcher. See Jean Flori, *Pierre l'Ermite et la première croisade* (Paris: Fayard, 1999).

13. Godfrey of Bouillon (1060–1100) was Duke of Lorraine and known for his great piety. He would become the first Latin ruler of Jerusalem in 1100. He did not take the title "king." See Pierre Aubé, *Godefroy de Bouillon* (Paris: Fayard, 1985).

14. Baldwin of Boulogne (died in 1118) was Godfrey's younger brother. After his older brother's death by plague, he was crowned the first Latin king of Jerusalem on Christmas Day 1100. See Paul Gindler, *Graf Balduin I von Edessa* (Halle: Kaemmerer, 1901).

15. Baldwin of Mons, or of Hainault (1058–1098). He died in battle against the Turks.

16. "Warriors" is a translation of the Latin *milites*, which is a difficult word to render into English. However, it does not mean "knight," which is a very loaded term and refers to a reality that is still about a hundred years in the future, in the context of the First Crusade.

17. The first use of the pronoun *I*, which suggests that the authors are using a source that may have been a brief firsthand account.

18. "Francia" under Charlemagne was a far bigger entity than mere France, stretching from the Spanish March to Carinthia in the east and down to Benevento in Italy.

19. This is the Via Egnatia, which ran from Durres in modern-day Albania all the way to Constantinople.

20. i.e., July 30.

21. Peter had been very active in the Rhineland. His People's Crusade consisted of men and women from France and Germany and Normans from Sicily and southern Italy.

22. i.e., Normans from Sicily and southern Italy.

23. Alexius I Comnenus (1056–1118) was crowned emperor of the Byzantine Empire on April 2, 1081.

24. "The Arm of Saint George" is the Bosporus Sea. A monastery, dedicated to Saint George, stood on Seraglio Point.

25. These various "evil deeds" are the result of the extreme poverty of these ordinary people who had come on the crusade with nothing but their fervor.

26. Modern-day Izmet in Turkey.

27. Nothing really is known of this Rainald other than what is related in the *Gesta*. He is not the same as Rainald of Broyes.

28. Romania is Asia Minor, or what the Turks called Rum, namely Rome. For the Greeks, Romania designated the totality of the Byzantine Empire.

29. Modern-day Iznik in Turkey.

30. This is Xerigordon, a fortified town near Nicaea.

31. September 29, 1096.

32. Rainald led an army of 6,000. Most were killed by the Turks after they were defeated; not many converted to Islam.

33. *Khorasan* is a general term for Persia, or perhaps a distant land, since Khorasan designated a vast area stretching out to the western portions of modern Afghanistan.

34. A city on the river Orontes, near present-day Antakya in Turkey.

35. In Syria.

36. Once mistakenly known as Walter the Penniless (because of a literal translation of his place of origin), Walter Sans-Avoir was a petty lord of Boissy-Sans-Avoir. He was killed in action in 1096, fighting the Turks.

37. Civetot (Kivotos) was a Greek port fortified by a castle on the gulf of Nicomedia (modern-day Izmet in Turkey).

38. On October 17, 1096, Peter had gone to Constantinople to get help from the emperor.

39. The number of men defeated was 20,000; most were slaughtered by the Turks.

40. Some 3,000 men fled into the castle of Civetot.

41. Not Iran, but Turkestan.

42. In fact, Peter the Hermit's plea for help worked, and the emperor did send a rescue force to Civetot and brought the survivors back to Constantinople.

43. The untrustworthiness of the Greeks is a theme that pervades all the crusade narratives and chronicles.

44. The second and third "parts" of the crusaders were the better organized and professionally led ones. This is the Princes' Crusade.

45. The land of the Croats and the Serbs; the former Yugoslavia.

46. Raymond IV of Toulouse (1042?–1105). He was the oldest and wealthiest of the various leaders of the crusade.

47. Adhemar of Monteil, who was bishop of Le Puy-en-Velay from 1082 until his death in 1098.

48. This is the Via Egnatia.

49. Bohemond (1058–1111) was the eldest son of Robert Guiscard and was the prince of Taranto and later the prince of Antioch.

50. Also known as Richard of Salerno (1060–1114); he was also Bohemond's cousin.

51. Robert II of Flanders (1065–1111); also known as Robert the Jerusalemite or Robert II of Jerusalem.

52. Robert Curthose (c. 1050–1134) was the eldest son of William the Conqueror.

53. Hugh I (1052–1101) was called "the Great," or "Magnus"; he was a son of Henry I of France.

54. Evrard III became the lord of Le Puiset and viscount of Chartres in 1064 after the death of his father. He likely died sometime in 1098 after the siege of Antioch, perhaps as a result of wounds.

55. Achard was from Trevoux, Ain, France.

56. A minor commander from Mouzon in the Ardenne.

57. These three Adriatic ports are in the region of Apulia.

58. William, the brother of Tancred, was Bohemond's nephew, being the son of his sister Emma and her husband Odo, called the Good Marquis.

59. This is John Comnenus (1073?–1106), son of Isaac the Sebastocrator, who was made the duke of Durres by his uncle the emperor Alexius I Comnenus.

60. Mounted Turkish archers who were employed by the Byzantine emperors.

61. A Turkish seminomadic people who were used in the Byzantine army.

62. These would be the poor foot soldiers in the crusader army, who often had no means to support themselves other than what they could scrounge.

63. This should not be confused with the modern town of Ponte di Scafari. Bohemond laid siege to the tower at the bridge of *scafati* (or boats), which spanned the Sarno River and defended the city of Amalfi. Bohemond was besieging the city sometime in June or July of 1096, along with his uncle Roger I of Sicily (1031–1101).

64. This is the Church of the Holy Sepulcher, which had been completely destroyed by the caliph Al-Hakim Abu Ali Mansur in 1009. After much negotiation, the Turks allowed the Byzantines to rebuild the church in 1048; as part of the agreement, the Byzantines opened a mosque in Constantinople. The rebuilt church was a lot smaller than the destroyed original; the Byzantines constructed as much as they could afford.

65. Bohemond left from Bari and landed at Valona, modern-day Vlorë in Albania.

66. Tancred (1072–1112) was the son of Odo the Good Marquis and Bohemond's nephew; he later became the Prince of Galilee.

67. Richard of Salerno (ca. 1160–1114) was Bohemond's cousin and the younger son of William of the Principate.

68. Rainulf of Salerno; another of Bohemond's cousins.

69. Little is known about Robert, perhaps the lord of Anse, a city on the river Saône.

70. Herman was the lord of Canny (modern-day Canny-sur-Matz). He likely died around 1110.

71. The lord of Sourdeval in Normandy who went to Sicily like many other Normans. His dates are not known. The last time he is heard from is as a witness to a charter made by Bohemond, dated July 14, 1098.

72. Nothing is known about Robert son of Tostain.

73. Nothing is known about Humphrey (Hunfredus).

74. Richard was the son of Rainulf of Salerno; see note 67 above.

75. There is some debate about the identity of this count. Perhaps his name was Geoffrey, and the names of his brothers were Gerard and Episcopus. As for Russinolo, it may refer either to Roussillon in Languedoc or to Roscignolo in the Principality of Salerno.

76. Nothing is known about Boel. However, he was likely the brother of the chronicler Fulcher of Chartres.

77. Nothing is known of Albered. He perhaps held the town of Cagnano (modern-day Cagnano Varano).

78. There seems to be an error in the manuscript. This cannot be Humphrey of Monte Scabioso, who was dead by 1096. Likely this should read, "Geoffrey of Monte Scabioso." Geoffrey was Humphrey's son, and therefore also Bohemond's relative. Monte Scabioso is a town in the Basilicata region of southern Italy.

79. The present-day city of Gjirokastër in southern Albania, which lies in the valley of the Drino River.

80. For the very first time, the narrative takes up the partisan view.

81. This is Kastoria, a city in northern Greece, which had a castle. Bohemond would know this area well, since the castle was taken by his father, Robert Guiscard, in 1082, during the five-year war (from 1080 to 1085) that Robert waged against the Byzantine emperor Alexius I Commenus. During this time, Bohemond was in charge of the campaign in northern Greece, and after being defeated by the emperor at Ioannina, he retreated to the castle at Kastoria, where the emperor pursued him. After a lengthy siege the castle fell in 1083 to the forces of the emperor.

82. No doubt the hostility toward Bohemond and his expedition stems fourteen years or so back.

83. This is the region of Pelagonia in Macedonia, the present-day Manastiri Prilep.

84. Either Bogomils or Manicheans.

85. The important subtext to such an action is Bohemond's previous military involvement in this area.

86. Vardar is a major river in Macedonia. It is also known by its Greek name, Axios.

87. Bohemond cannot antagonize the emperor.

88. Ash Wednesday, February 18, 1097.

THE SECOND NARRATIVE

1. Curopalate was an early Byzantine noble title usually granted to members of the royal family. However, by the time of the First Crusade, the function had been considerably downgraded to being a mere functionary of the royal court.

2. The term *iusticia terre* in the origin refers to the immunity given to all Christian territory, which was not to be attacked by the crusaders.

3. A city in eastern Macedonia; it had a Byzantine castle.

4. February 18.

5. This is the ancient Greek and Byzantine city of Rhusion, modern-day Topiris on the river Mesta.

6. April 1, 1096.

7. The basis of this objection is the fact that the only oath the crusaders took as pilgrims was a holy one before God alone. The emperor seeks to change pilgrimage into political allegiance to him.

8. An important insight into the dynamics of the crusaders—the resentment felt by the common warrior, who sees the highborn as being motivated by selfish reasons. Like the theme of the untrustworthy Greeks, the theme of the relationship of the classes, with the highborn protecting their own interests to the detriment of the rest, is a recurrent one in the various crusade chronicles.

9. This refers to the attacks on the Byzantine Empire during 1080–1085 by Bohemond and his father, Robert Guiscard. See note 81 in narrative 1.

10. Once again, a manifestation of the theme of the relationship of the classes.

11. Swearing allegiance to Alexius was a serious dilemma for many crusaders, since it meant a form of vassalage.

12. The old road was a heavily wooded and narrow track that led through deep ravines and required crossing the Orontes River some twenty times.

13. These are the participants in the People's Crusade earlier led by Peter the Hermit.

14. This is likely the Katirli Dagi.

15. Wednesday, May 6, 1097.

16. The physical hardships of the crusaders are often overlooked. Hunger was a never-ending problem, and many among the poorer contingent of the crusading army starved to death.

17. May 14, 1097.

18. Typical siege weapons at the time of the First Crusade were various types of catapults and siege towers, which allowed men to be delivered safely to the top of a city wall for deployment and engagement with the enemy.

19. Sapping walls was a common strategy of the time.

20. An auxiliary contingent of Turks.

21. The logistics of besieging and rendering a city is a subject often ignored in crusade studies.

22. Located to the south and southeast of the city of Nicaea.

23. Fear was one of the major factors of a city's surrender.

24. Stephen (1045–1102) was the count of Blois, of Châteaudun, of Chartres, of Meaux, and lord of Sancerre. He did not have a very high reputation

among the crusaders because of his eventual desertion at the siege of Antioch and his return back home.

25. Roger was lord of Barneville (modern-day Barneville Carteret). He accompanied William the Conqueror in 1066 to England and was given substantial grants of land. When the First Crusade was declared, he went in the contingent of Duke Robert Curthose (William's eldest son). Roger died in 1098 at the battle of Antioch. He is also mentioned in Torquato Tasso's *Jerusalem Delivered*, canto I, stanza 54.

26. All the crusaders fought together.

27. Modern-day Lake Iznik, which covers an area of around 290 square meters.

28. The casualties were very high.

29. The white stole of martyrdom. Cf. Revelation 7:9 (After these things I looked, and behold, a great multitude which no one could count, from every nation and all tribes and peoples and tongues, standing before the throne and before the Lamb, clothed in white robes, and palm branches were in their hands).

30. Cf. Revelation 6:10 (and they cried out with a loud voice, saying, How long, O Lord, holy and true, will You refrain from judging and avenging our blood on those who dwell on the earth?).

THE THIRD NARRATIVE

1. That is, Nicaea. The crusaders departed on June 28, 1097.

2. A bridge over the Göksu river. It was known as the Saleph River during the time of the First Crusade. Frederick Barbarossa drowned in it in 1190 (during the Third Crusade).

3. Angulani are Arabs from Sicily and North Africa. The term stems from the Greek 'αγαρηνοί, meaning "the sons of Hagar," which refers back to the origin myth of the Muslim Arabs who claimed descent from Ishmael, the son of Abraham and Hagar. See Genesis 16 and 21.

4. Paulicians were adoptionists who believed that God adopted Jesus at the time of the latter's baptism. Paulicians were frequently found in Armenia. However, for the author of the *Gesta* the term *Paulician* seems to be exoticism for anyone non-Christian.

5. The battle began around 8 a.m. and ended around 2 p.m.

6. There is a deep-seated respect for the martial prowess of the Turks.

THE FOURTH NARRATIVE

1. Suleiman II (or Kilij Arslan I) was the sultan of Rum; he was the commander of Turkish forces at the battle of Dorylaeum. He died in 1107; his birth date is not known. "Suleiman the Old" is Suleiman ibn Qutulmish, his father, who established the Sultanate of Rum in Anatolia; he died in 1086.

2. The speech of the Muslim characters in the *Gesta* tends to be exotic; perhaps an attempt by the author to capture the florid formality of eastern courtly speech? The Arabs had come to help him but dispersed when they learned that he had been defeated.

3. An interesting parallel to the astonishment of the crusaders earlier at the number of Turks crowding the hills and valleys.

4. Armenian Christians.

5. The custom of kidnapping Christian male children was common among the Turks; such children were raised to become warriors, such as the later and famous Janissaries; the *Gesta* gives us a very early record of this practice.

6. This is the arid Anatolian Plateau, which sees hardly any rainfall during the summer months.

7. Cactus and aloe plants that grow in this region.

8. Present-day Konya in Turkey.

9. Mostly Armenians.

10. The waterskin; a common method of carrying a large quantity of water in the east.

11. The Çarşamba-Su, which is the only substantial body of water near Konya.

12. Heraclea Cybistra, not far from the modern-day city of Ereğli.

13. Modern-day Bozanta, out toward the coast of Cilicia (Çukurova).

14. The major city of Cilicia, the birthplace of Saint Paul.

15. Athena is Adana, not far from the Mediterranean Sea and located on the banks of the river Seyhan. Manustra is the ancient city of Mamistra, also located on the river Seyhan. Tancred got these cities around the end of September or early October.

16. This is Lesser Armenia, part of the Armenian plateau.

17. Likely a minor Armenian prince.

18. Caesarea is modern-day Kayseri in the Turkish province of Kayseri. Cappadocia is the ancient name for the central region of Turkey.

19. The ancient city of Comana in Cappadocia.

20. It is difficult to know who exactly this crusader is. In the *Gesta* his name is given as Petrus de Alpibus. The usual identification is Peter of Aulps, a

Provençal nobleman. However, "Alpibus" may also be rendered as "Alfia," thus making him a Norman or Frenchman from Italy. Lastly, he is also referred to as Petrus Francigena, "Peter the son of a Frank."

21. Peter became lord of Comana around October 3, 1097.

22. This is the ancient city of Cocussus, present-day Göksun in the Mediterranean part of Turkey.

23. It was an Armenian city at this time.

24. Either Castillon or Châtillon; both common names in France. Perhaps Castillon in the Gironde, given the fact that he is one of Raymond of Toulouse's men. Another possibility is that he might belong to the Châtillon family, whose members included such famous men as Raynald of Châtillon and Walter of Châtillon. But all this can only be conjecture. Nothing is really known about Peter of Castellione.

25. William of Montpellier (1075–1121) was the fifth lord of Montpellier. He returned to France after the First Crusade.

26. It is likely that Roasa does not refer to the village of Roaix in the Vaucluse region of southern France, as has been commonly suggested. Perhaps it is Peter of Roas. Nothing further is known about Peter other than what we are told in the *Gesta*.

27. Peter Raymond of Hautpoul; he died in 1098 of the plague.

28. This has been misidentified as Riha (modern-day Şanlıurfa). Rather, it is Al-Ruj, the area around the Orontes River and Jabal al-Summaq.

29. This has been accepted as Ruweha, an important Christian center. However, the identification is not tenable. Rather, it is likely that "Rusa" is Al-Arus or Allaruz. And Qastun is also a very strong possibility.

30. One of the peaks of the Anti-Taurus Mountains.

31. Present-day Kahramanmaraş, which is located at the foot of the Taurus Mountains.

32. This is Syrian Antioch, or Antioch on the Orontes. The modern Turkish city of Antakya is close by.

THE FIFTH NARRATIVE

1. This is a notoriously problematic reference in the *Gesta*. The common mistake is to try to make sense of the term, given the fact that bridges made of iron did not exist at the time. Hence the original *pontem ferreum* or *farreum* is taken to mean "the bridge of Far." And then "the Far" is often noted as being "Farfar," a local name for the Orontes. Again, this is a misidentification, since the *Gesta* does later call the Orontes Farfar, and therefore the bridge would then

properly be referred to as *pons Farfareum*, since the author of the *Gesta* is familiar with this alternative name for the Orontes. Incidentally, there is another Farfar (or Pharphar) near Damascus (see 2 Kings 5:12), and it is likely that the medieval references to the Orontes as the Farfar might stem from misplaced biblical geography. Nor should "Farfar" be taken to be a Latinization of some local name for the Orontes. Rather, *pontem ferreum* is a direct translation of the name of an actual bridge that spanned the river Ifrin, some twenty miles north of Antioch. It was known locally as *Jisr-al-Hadid*, literally, "the bridge of iron," and consisted of nine arches. The term *al-hadid* is figurative and means "enduring," "strong," although it must be noted that the two gates on the bridge were known to have iron braces. A very famous battle was fought on this bridge between the Byzantines and the caliph Umar in 637 AD. The iron bridge lasted well into the twentieth century, when it was torn down. It should also be noted that the city of Antioch had an entrance known as the Iron Gate, though the gate was made of wood. Incidentally, there is the ancient city of Karkar (Qarqar), which is located in the Orontes river valley and which was inhabited during the time of the First Crusade. If a nonbiblical source for the name "Farfar" is needed (though unlikely), perhaps it might be suggested that "Farfar" is a corrupt form of *Karkar*. However, tracing and then explaining consonantal shifts, especially in place-names, is often a dead end.

2. The Orontes.

3. That is, October 21, 1097.

4. This is the castle of Harim, or Harenc.

5. A phrase that means a Christian martyr.

6. This is the first mention of the crusaders building a castle; probably more a fort than a castle. It was built just north of the city. "Maregard" is *malregard*, likely a nickname given to a mountain by the crusaders. The term means "the evil eye"—soldiers' superstition to ward off the evil eye?

7. December 28, 1098.

8. An allusion to Romans 9:22 (What if God, although willing to demonstrate His wrath and to make His power known, endured with much patience vessels of wrath prepared for destruction?).

THE SIXTH NARRATIVE

1. The name of the seneschal is not known. The bishop's banner had an image of the Virgin of Puy on it.

2. The Orontes.

3. This would be the name later given to Mount Habib Neccar to the east by the crusaders. It would be called "Tancred's mountain" only sometime after April 1098 when Tancred guarded a castle on it.

4. This is the hyperpyron, the Byzantine gold coin recently introduced in 1092, following monetary reform by Alexius I. It had a very high standard of purity—about 20.5 carats—and therefore quickly became the standard against which all other currency was measured.

5. William "the Carpenter" was the viscount of Melun. He earned his nickname because of his ferocity in battle; he hacked down men like a carpenter hacking away at wood. He is also known for desertion. He appears in history ca. 1085, and nothing further is known about him after 1101.

6. This is a reference to William's desertion of his men in Spain in 1087 during a campaign against the Moors of Spain. William abandoned his men and fled into France, resulting in the deaths of many.

7. The Latin term *Frankigenae* is a specific reference to those crusaders who are from the Île-de-France region of France and therefore the fellow countrymen of William. This is why they intercede on his behalf. Regional affiliations were fundamental to medieval social organization, which is why the modern idea of France did not exist. People were regional rather than national.

8. And he returned to Melun. However, he returned to the Holy Land in the minor crusade of 1101, in which those who had remained behind and those who had turned back could have the opportunity to become crusaders. It is likely that he returned to Antioch and served Bohemond.

9. Tetigus was a Byzantine commander of Turkish descent. In the various accounts of the First Crusade he is reviled as a liar and as a deserter. It is unsure as to why he left the siege with promise of bringing help. Perhaps it was a ploy to get away, since he was greatly disliked by the crusaders.

10. It seems that Bohemond spread the rumor that he was a liar who had no intention of coming back with help and provisions for the crusaders.

11. The desertions were very high, especially among the poor contingents of the crusaders who had to forage as best they could.

12. Lake Antioch or El Bahr. It was completely drained in the 1970s to reclaim further land, with dire environmental consequences to this day.

13. The son of Gerard count of Buonalbergo and Ariano (obit 1085), Robert was another of Bohemond's cousins and his closest companion, being both his standard-bearer and constable. He returned to southern Italy sometime in 1112 and was a close supporter of his nephew and new lord, Count Jordan. He disappears from history after 1119.

14. *Hoc bellum non est carnale, sed spirituale* is a succinct summary of the very ethic of the crusades.

15. A vivid biblical allusion. Cf. Hosea 13:8 (I will encounter them like a bear robbed of her cubs, and I will tear open their chests; there I will also devour them like a lioness, as a wild beast would tear them).

16. Bohemond's banner was supposedly red in color with a representation of a serpent.

17. This suggests the extent of the route in that the crusaders chased the Turks for over twenty miles, which is the distance to the bridge of iron from Antioch.

18. The crusaders referred to Cairo as Babylon, which was ruled by the Fatimids. The emir at this time was Al-Mustali (obit 1101). The Fatimids were dire enemies of the Turks. The delegation had come to work out an alliance with the crusaders against the Turks.

19. Shrove Tuesday, February 9, 1098.

THE SEVENTH NARRATIVE

1. A vague reference, meaning various eastern lands.

2. It is not clear how many gates the medieval city of Antioch had. Estimates range from five to ten or even eleven. The mosque was located in the western part of the city, facing the Sea Gate; it had a Muslim cemetery.

3. The port of Saint Symeon in Seleucia Pieria (modern-day Samandağ) was located at the mouth of the Orontes and served as the major port of Antioch. It lay about seventeen miles from the city.

4. Important insight into the use of labor during the First Crusade; sailors would have the necessary tools to construct walls (pulleys, ropes, winches). Earlier, at port Symeon, the Genoese had brought in thirteen ships with supplies (which arrived on November 7, 1098). On March 4, 1098, a fleet of ships from England had arrived with supplies.

5. March 5, 1098.

6. The bridge that faced the Bridge Gate. It survived until the 1960s.

7. Cf. Matthew 25:41 (Then He will also say to those on His left, "Depart from Me, accursed ones, into the eternal fire which has been prepared for the devil and his angels").

8. The mosque.

9. Port of Saint Symeon. This also suggests that the crusaders had an amiable meeting with the emir's delegation.

10. An accurate description of how dressed stone would be obtained.

THE EIGHTH NARRATIVE

1. The castle was next to the monastery of Saint George on the left bank of the Orontes.

2. Cf. John 21:25 (And there are also many other things which Jesus did, which if they were written in detail, I suppose that even the world itself would not contain the books that would be written).

3. Perhaps a Latinized version of the Persian name Pirouz. Turks often took on Persian names.

4. Such friendships warn us not to read crusade narratives in black-and-white terms.

5. Rather a technical word meaning a nonbeliever. It's a Greek pejorative term that means "unleavened ones" and refers to an obscure dispute between Latin and Orthodox believers. The Latin Christians celebrated Holy Communion with unleavened bread, while the Greek Church favored leavened bread.

6. The land of the Saracens lay to the east and to the south.

7. That is, from the southwest.

8. Perhaps an ordinary name, or perhaps a nickname. It also had a strict legal meaning—a priest who has abused his office. So, perhaps the foot soldier is a defrocked priest? The term *malacorona* means "ill-tonsured." There is evidence for this nickname in eleventh century Normandy: Roger Malacorona in Caen and Raoul Malacorona, the uncle of Robert of Grandmesnil.

9. A Greek phrase, μικρους Φράγκους 'έχομεν. This suggests that the language of common parlance was Greek, although some crusaders also knew Arabic.

10. That is, a Norman from southern Italy.

11. The citadel stood on Mount Silpius behind an enclosure, which the crusaders failed to take.

12. This is Yaghi-Siyan, the Turkish governor of Antioch. "Cassian" is a rendition of "Siyan."

13. The area to the west of the enclosure guarded by Tancred.

14. A casal is a village of tenant farmers.

15. A Byzantine gold coin with a very high value.

16. Thursday, June 3, 1098.

THE NINTH NARRATIVE

1. This is Kür-Bogha, or Kerbogha, the governor of Mosul (Iraq).

2. That is, Barkiyaruq, the sultan of the Turkish nation. His empire spanned most of modern-day Middle East and Central Asia.

3. That is, Al-Mustadhir (1078–1118) who was the caliph in Baghdad. The Turks recognized him as a spiritual leader only; he was politically irrelevant at the time.

4. This might be Muineddin Sökmen (obit 1105), or it could be his brother Ilghazi (obit 1122), since both of them had held Jerusalem. However, in 1098, Al-Afdal Shahanshah (1066–1121) had just captured Jerusalem from Ilghazi. So the reference might be to him also.

5. This is the Turkish ruler Duqaq, who governed Damascus from 1095–1104. He was the son of the famous Tutush.

6. A Latinized version of Shams-ud-Dawla.

7. By "castle" the citadel is meant. The *Gesta* does confuse the two. This type of "inside information" is perhaps the result of intelligence received from uplᴜᴜ ᴵⁿ ᴛʰᴜ Tᴜʀᴋᴵᴜʜ ᴊᴀᴍᴘ.

8. Again, the citadel is meant.

9. The Karasu and the Orontes rivers.

10. That is, the citadel.

11. That is, the citadel.

12. Again, the confusion in terminology; although it is properly used here after the various references to "the castle."

13. A rather western cultural reference. The "rivers" of the Amazons, in classical mythology, were the Terme (Thermodon in Greek) and the Iris. Themiscyra, the capital city of the Amazons, was located in the plains between these two rivers.

14. The assumption is that Muslims are polytheists.

15. By the time of the First Crusade, Bulgaria was thoroughly part of the Byzantine Empire, the era of the First Bulgarian Empire well over a hundred years behind.

16. Apulia was the seat of Norman power in southern Italy at this time, and from where many of the crusaders with Bohemond originated.

17. That is, Aleppo, in northern Syria.

18. Earlier, Bohemond had been compared to a raging lion.

19. This is also very reminiscent of the warning sent to Pilate by his wife concerning Jesus: "While he was sitting on the judgment seat, his wife sent him a message, saying, 'Have nothing to do with that righteous Man; for last night I suffered greatly in a dream because of Him'" (Matthew 27:19). Like Curbaram, Pilate ignores the warning.

20. The mother proceeds to give an intricate homily, very much like the one found at the beginning of the First Narrative.

21. Psalm 68:30 (He has scattered the peoples who delight in war).

22. Psalm 79:6 (Pour out Your wrath upon the nations which do not know You, and upon the kingdoms which do not call upon Your name).

23. Matthew 9:15 (And Jesus said to them, "The attendants of the bridegroom cannot mourn as long as the bridegroom is with them, can they? But

the days will come when the bridegroom is taken away from them, and then they will fast [*filii sponsi* in the Vulgate, 'sons of the Bridegroom']").

24. Galatians 4:1–7 (Now I say, as long as the heir is a child, he does not differ at all from a slave although he is owner of everything, but he is under guardians and managers until the date set by the father. So also we, while we were children, were held in bondage under the elemental things of the world. But when the fullness of the time came, God sent forth His Son, born of a woman, born under the Law, so that He might redeem those who were under the Law, that we might receive the adoption as sons. Because you are sons, God has sent forth the Spirit of His Son into our hearts, crying, "Abba! Father!" Therefore you are no longer a slave, but a son; and if a son, then an heir through God), and Romans 9:8 (That is, it is not the children of the flesh who are children of God, but the children of the promise are regarded as descendants).

25. Romans 8:17 (and if children, heirs also, heirs of God and fellow heirs with Christ, if indeed we suffer with Him so that we may also be glorified with Him).

26. A mixture of Psalm 113:3 (From the rising of the sun to its setting the name of the Lord is to be praised); Isaiah 45:6 (That men may know from the rising to the setting of the sun that there is no one besides Me. I am the Lord, and there is no other); Malachi 1:11 ("For from the rising of the sun even to its setting, My name will be great among the nations, and in every place incense is going to be offered to My name, and a grain offering that is pure; for My name will be great among the nations," says the Lord of hosts); Deuteronomy 11:24–25 (Every place on which the sole of your foot treads shall be yours; your border will be from the wilderness to Lebanon, and from the river, the river Euphrates, as far as the western sea. No man will be able to stand before you; the Lord your God will lay the dread of you and the fear of you on all the land on which you set foot, as He has spoken to you); and Joshua 1:4–5 (From the wilderness and this Lebanon, even as far as the great river, the river Euphrates, all the land of the Hittites, and as far as the Great Sea toward the setting of the sun will be your territory. No man will be able to stand before you all the days of your life. Just as I have been with Moses, I will be with you; I will not fail you or forsake you).

27. That is, the Koran.

28. Belief in astrology was an important aspect of science in Turkish culture, and royal court astrologer (*müneccimbaşi*) was a position of very high rank.

29. This is a euhemeristic explanation of the prowess of both Bohemond and Tancred. But according to the logic of the *Gesta* it makes sense, since Curbaram is a polytheist and prone to seeing gods in human form. A curious way to compliment Bohemond and Tancred.

30. Cf. Isaiah 47:4 (Our Redeemer—the Lord Almighty is His name—is the Holy One of Israel); New International Version; 1984.

31. Exodus 20:11 (For in six days the Lord made the heavens and the earth, the sea and all that is in them, and rested on the seventh day; therefore the Lord blessed the Sabbath day and made it holy); Psalm 146:6 (Who made heaven and earth, the sea and all that is in them; Who keeps faith forever).

32. Cf. Psalm 45:6 (Your throne, O God, is forever and ever; a scepter of uprightness is the scepter of Your kingdom).

33. Cf. Psalm 89:7 (God greatly feared in the council of the holy ones, and awesome above all those who are around Him).

34. Rather a humorous practicality after the lengthy homily.

35. That is, the citadel, already held by the Turks.

36. Thursday, June 10, 1098.

37. William of Grandmesnil (ca. 1055–1060 to ca. 1100–1114) was a Norman baron from Calabria; he was the son of Hugh of Grandmesnil (who was a companion of William the Conqueror and given extensive lands in Lincolnshire). William returned to Calabria after the First Crusade.

38. This is Aubrey of Grandmesnil; there was a third brother with them, Ivo of Grandmesnil.

39. Guy de Montlhéry was the lord of Montlhéry in Île-de-France. "Trousseau" was likely a nickname.

40. Lambert was the count of Clermont. He was nicknamed "the Poor." He returned to France and died sometime around 1147.

41. Another prominent "fugitive" was Stephen Count of Blois, whose wife was Adela (daughter of William the Conqueror) and to whom he wrote many letters describing his exploits. She forced him to return to the Holy Land to complete his pilgrimage, and he took part in the minor crusade of 1101. He was killed at the battle of Ramleh in 1102.

42. In the city of Antioch.

43. This wall was inside the city.

44. The crusaders had had no time to gather supplies and prepare for a siege. Kerbogha had come upon them suddenly.

45. Perhaps named Stephen Valentine.

46. This strangely or carelessly has been misindentified by some of the editors and translators of the *Gesta*. "They are assembled" refers to the First Response, Second Nocturne for the first Sunday in October. The entire Response runs as follows: *Congregati sunt inimici nostri et gloriantur in virtute sua: contere fortitudinem illorum, Domine, et disperge illos, ut cognoscant quia non est alius qui pugnet pro nobis nisi tu, Deus noster* (Our enemies have gathered and they glory in their might: destroy their strength, O Lord, and scatter them,

that they may know there is none who fights for us, but you, our God). The words (from the Catholic Bible) are taken from 1 Maccabees 3:52–53; Ecclesiasticus (The Book of Sirach) 36:5; Exodus 14:14, 25; Deuteronomy 1:30; Joshua 10:14, 23:3; and Psalm 58:12. And "the verse" is the minor doxology: *Gloria Patri, et Filio, et Spiritui Sancto. Sicut erat in principio, et nunc, et semper, et in saecula saeculorum. Amen* (Glory be to the Father, and to the Son, and to the Holy Ghost. As it was in the beginning, is now, and ever shall be; world without end. Amen).

47. This is Peter Bartholomaeus, who claimed to have had five visions of St. Andrew. He was perhaps a monk and ranked among the poor, impoverished crusaders. His claim of having discovered at Antioch the lance that pierced Jesus was thoroughly doubted, especially by Adhemar, the bishop of Puy and most other noblemen (likely because many of them would know of the Holy Lance in Constantinople, housed at the Church of the Virgin of the Pharos since the mid-tenth century). Despite the fact that the "discovery" of the lance at Antioch had heartened and strengthened a demoralized and starving crusader army, most did not believe it was authentic. To prove the doubters wrong, Peter went through an ordeal by fire, holding the lance in his hand. As he walked through the flames, he claimed he saw Jesus. He died some twelve days later, on April 20, 1099, from the burns he had suffered.

48. The Cave-Church of Saint Peter in Antioch; perhaps it is mentioned in Acts 11:25–27 (And he left for Tarsus to look for Saul; and when he had found him, he brought him to Antioch and for an entire year they met with the church and taught considerable numbers; and the disciples were first called Christians in Antioch. Now at this time some prophets came down from Jerusalem to Antioch).

49. Cf. Psalm 106:44 (Nevertheless He looked upon their distress when He heard their cry).

50. That is, the citadel. Again the confusion between "castle" and "citadel" in the original.

51. Again, the citadel.

52. Nothing is known about this Hugh. And Gosfred is Geoffrey of Monte Scabioso, who was killed earlier at the battle of Dorylaeum. The *Gesta* does confuse his name thoroughly; earlier he was called by his father's name, "Hunfredus," or Humphrey, then later "Godefridus," or Godfrey, and now "Gosfredus" or "Goffredus." All three instances refer to the same person, namely, Geoffrey of Monte Scabioso.

53. The original reads, *in castellum* ("into the castle"). But that would be impossible, since the castle/citadel was held by the Turks. Perhaps they ran toward the citadel and to the mountains behind it.

54. This figure simply implies, "very many houses and churches." As an old Christian center, Antioch had many old churches and monasteries.

55. That is, the citadel.

56. The fighting was too intense to allow for any rest.

57. To stop the Turks in the citadel from attacking inside the city.

58. In the valley of Mount Cassius.

59. There was a low-latitude aurora. There had been other natural "portents": an earthquake at Edessa (December 30, 1098), this aurora, and then pouring rain and dropping temperatures.

60. ⟨illegible⟩

61. A fool because of his desertion and his return home to France, and because he convinced Alexius not to send help to the besieged crusaders at Antioch, since it was all hopeless.

62. The port city of Alexandretta (present-day Iskenderun), located about forty miles north of Antioch.

63. Present-day city of Akşehir, in Konya province, in central Turkey.

64. Guy of Hauteville (ca. 1061–1108) was with the emperor's army in 1098. He was Bohemond's half-brother.

65. Showing emotions and shedding tears was not considered unmanly in the Middle Ages.

66. This conveys the inherent shock felt by the crusaders that God would let down His own people and allow them to be defeated at Antioch. This is a time of profound doubt and a blow to individual faith.

67. Guy is the only one not convinced by Stephen's testimony.

68. This may well be the Echmiadzin lance now in the Vatican.

69. Nothing is known of this Herluin; he might have been a priest.

70. An antithesis of sorts to Curbaram's mother's words earlier.

71. The other language would be Turkish.

72. The one found by Peter Bartholomaeus.

73. From the citadel.

74. In the northwest section of the city.

75. Kilij Arslan, who was the sultan of Rum.

76. Perhaps Rainald of Toul, or of Beauvais. Nothing further is known about him.

77. In Byzantine iconography, these saints are shown as warrior-saints; and Saint George was the patron saint of the crusaders.

78. This incident is only mentioned in the *Gesta*.

79. That is, the Normans from southern Italy.

80. June 28, 1098.

THE TENTH NARRATIVE

1. This is because Bohemond had a violent quarrel with the other counts about taking sole possession of Antioch. The counts wanted to give the city to the emperor Alexius. Hugh does not return because Alexius did not want to escalate the problem.

2. That is, November 1, 1098.

3. In fact, many thought this to be a poor decision, which is why many set off to pursue their own adventures while they waited out the summer.

4. Raymond Pilet or Pelet (1075–1143) belonged to the ancient and eminent house of Narbonne-Pelet in Languedoc. Through marriage he was lord of Alais. He was a much-celebrated hero of the First Crusade.

5. This is the village of Tel-Mannas in Syria.

6. This is Ma`ârra an-Nu`mân, a village in Syria, located along the road to Aleppo.

7. This date is wrong. It should be July 27, 1098.

8. Of Tel-Mannas.

9. That is, Raymond Pilet.

10. August 1, 1098. Bishop Adhemar likely died of typhus. He was buried in the church of Saint Peter in Antioch. Afterward, Peter Bartholomaeus had his revenge of sorts, for he reported that the bishop had appeared to him in a dream and had told him that he had been sent down into Hell because he doubted the veracity of the lance found by Peter. But Christ had taken pity on him and brought him up to Heaven.

11. This is the small city of Al-Bara, which was an important place in its time, with several churches, monasteries, and a bishop. Raymond removed the Turkish overlords.

12. A mosque.

13. This was Pierre of Narbonne, who was known for his saintliness.

14. That is, November 1, 1098.

15. This chiefly refers to the arguments, often bitter and violent, over Antioch with Bohemond.

16. That is, the cost he incurred in liberating Antioch, and which would then give him a right over it, according to his view.

17. There was further hostility between Bohemond and the count of Saint-Gilles.

18. The two summits of Mount Silpius, Mount Stauris, and Mount Casius.

19. This is the citadel, built on a ridge of Mount Silpius.

20. This is John the Oxite, who consecrated Peter of Narbonne as bishop of Antioch.

21. The walls were Byzantine, built sometime after 540 AD.

22. The medieval name for the Orontes.

23. This is, of course, pure myth-making.

24. This is true. Antioch was founded in the fourth century BC by Seleucus I, who named the city after his father, Antiochus.

25. That is, Al-Ruj.

26. It was already taken by the count of Saint-Gilles.

27. A city that Raymond Pilet could not capture.

28. "Counts" is a mistake on the part of the authors of the *Gesta*. Only one count was involved in the attack on Marra—Raymond, count of Saint-Gilles. Bohemond joined up with Raymond. "Counts" is retained in this translation to point to the fact that the authors of the *Gesta* assume this thing up.

29. Nothing is known about this Evrard. Perhaps he was known as "the Hunter" because he had brought along his hunting horn, which he blew before or during the attack. This calls to mind the hunting horn carried by Lt. Col. John Dutton Frost during the Battle of Arnhem in World War II.

30. The Turks and Arabs did not have the knowledge to make Greek fire, which was a Byzantine state secret. Here, burning arrows are meant to be those the defenders are shooting at the crusaders.

31. Perhaps this refers to Golfier of Lastours. "Daturre" could be a misreading of Lastours by the author of the *Gesta*. Golfier of Lastours was the lord of Lastours and perhaps the brother of Gregory Bechada, who wrote the *The Canso Antioca*, an account of the First Crusade, which now only exists as a brief fragment. As well, there is the famous Golfier legend, which relates the story of a lion that was being strangled by a snake until Golfier came to its rescue. The lion became a devoted pet and helped him in many a battle. When Golfier returned home, he had to leave the lion behind, but the animal jumped into the sea and swam behind the ship on which Golfier was sailing. But in the end its strength gave out, and it drowned. This legend is first told in the chronicle of Jaufré de Vigeois, which was completed around 1184.

32. It is unclear which palace this might be, but it is likely a *konak*, or an official residence.

33. William the bishop of Orange died around December 20, 1098.

34. One of the most infamous incidents of the First Crusade.

35. The feud between Bohemond and Raymond continues.

36. An expression of piety, since crusaders perceived themselves to be pilgrims bound for Jerusalem. But perhaps also a way to garner support.

37. Present-day Kafartab in Syria.

38. Present-day Shaizar (Saijar). Caesarea is a misnomer, because the crusaders assumed it was Kayseri, or Caesarea Mazaca.

39. "The king," or more properly emir of Shaizar at this time, was Ali ibn Munqidh, the uncle of the famous Usama ibn Munqidh.

40. Near the Orontes, and near the town of Hamah.

41. It is not possible to identify this castle; it would lie between Shaizar and Hamah.

42. That is, the Koran.

43. This is likely Masyaf castle.

44. Likely an emir belonging to the Mirdasid dynasty.

45. This is perhaps a misreading by the authors of the *Gesta* for Rafaniya, which lay along the road to Tripoli.

46. One of the peaks in the Nusayri mountain range.

47. Likely the Bukaya plain; there, atop one of the hills, is located the majestic Krak des Chevaliers.

48. This is the Kurdish castle that would later become the famed Krak des Chevaliers.

49. February 2, 1099.

50. This is the city of Homs or Hims. In Latin sources it is called Camela, which means a "she-camel."

51. This was the Qazi of Tripoli, Fakhr al-Mulk Abû 'Ali ibn'Ammâ; he was able to remain in Tripoli as ruler until 1109, when Tancred finally captured the city.

52. The present-day site of Tell-Arqa, which was ruled by the Qazi of Tripoli. The name of the city was also linked biblically by the crusaders as being the city founded by Aracaeus, the nephew of Noah. Cf. Genesis 10:17.

53. Tripoli is now the capital of Libya.

54. This is Raymond of Turenne (1074–1137), the viscount of Turenne in the Bas-Limousin, France.

55. Both the Raymonds were part of the army of Raymond, count of Saint-Gilles.

56. Modern-day Tartus, Syria.

57. One of the few times that the Gesta uses the term *host* for the entire crusader army.

58. That is, Maraqiyah, just north of Tartus.

59. The modern-day port city of Latakia, Syria.

60. Modern-day Jableh, a small port city lying between Latakia and Tartus.

61. This is perhaps the qazi Abu Mohammed Obaidullah.

62. Likely the Nahr Arka.

63. April 10, 1099.

64. Likely the port city of Tartus.

65. Anselm of Ostrevent was the lord of Ribemont; he was known as "the Bearded." He was killed around February 25, 1099. He is the author of two letters to Manasses II, the archbishop of Rheims.

66. Nothing is known about William. Likely, he was part of Anselm's contingent from Picardy.

67. That is, the Qazi of Tripoli, Fakhr al-Mulk Abû 'Ali ibn'Ammâ.

68. Monday, May 16, 1099.

69. That is, Batroun, Lebanon.

70. That is, Byblos or Jbeil, Lebanon.

71. The Nahr Ibrahim, just south of Byblos. In antiquity it was known as the river of Adonis.

72. May 19, 1099.

73. Beirut, Lebanon.

74. Present-day Sidon, Lebanon.

75. Modern-day Tyre, Lebanon.

76. Acre, Israel, on the Bay of Haifa.

77. Likely the modern-day city of Haifa, which was thought to be named after Caiaphas, the high priest of the Sanhedrin, before whom Jesus was judged.

78. That is, Ramla, Israel.

79. The Byzantine church of Saint George in Lydda (or now Lod, Israel) was destroyed by the Arabs, and the crusaders rebuilt it from ruins. This church in turn was again destroyed by the Muslims under Saladin. A new church was not rebuilt until the late nineteenth century.

80. This was Robert of Rouen, who was involved in building a new church and reorganizing the area. This was likely in conjunction with the Orthodox Church.

81. June 7 rather than June 6, 1099.

82. The church of Saint Stephen in Jerusalem was destroyed and rebuilt several times, but each time it likely stood on the place where the present-day church of Saint Etienne (Stephen) now stands.

83. Around the area where the Benedictine abbey of Hagia Maria Sion now stands.

84. This is Raymond of Turenne. The *Gesta* confuses his name; he was called Raymond of Tentoria earlier.

85. Monday, June 13, 1099.

86. The pool of Siloam was where Jesus healed the blind man. It is located to the south of the old city of Jerusalem. See John 9:7 (And [Jesus] said to him, "Go, wash in the pool of Siloam" [which is translated, Sent]. So he went away and washed, and came back seeing).

87. A fleet of Genoese ships in Jaffa, Israel.

88. The port city of Jaffa.

89. From Trevoux, Ain, France.

90. William (1055–1105) was the lord of Sabran in the Gard region of France.

91. Saturday, July 9, 1099; or perhaps Sunday, July 10.

92. Wednesday, July 13, and Thursday, July 14, 1099.

93. Friday, July 15, 1099.

94. Eustace of Boulogne (1060–1125).

95. He was from Tournai, Belgium.

96. Where the mosque of Omar now stands.

97. Perhaps Iftikhar-ud-Daula.

98. A tower near the Jaffa Gate.

99. The Al-Aqsa mosque.

100. Likely Gaston viscount of Béarn in the Pyrenees. He died around 1131.

101. Ashkelon in southern Israel.

102. August 1, 1099.

103. August 1, 1099. Arnulf of Chocques was the chaplain of Duke Robert Curthose of Normandy. He was the first Latin Patriarch of Jerusalem. He died in 1118.

104. Friday, July 15, 1099.

105. Modern-day Nablus in the West Bank.

106. Godfrey of Bouillon.

107. That is, Cairo, Egypt. The emir was Al-Mustali.

108. August 9, 1099.

109. Arnold the bishop of Martirano in Catanzaro province, Calabria, Italy.

110. August 10, 1099.

111. That is, the Holy Sepulcher.

112. Likely the Nahr-as-Safiya that runs between Ashkelon and Jerusalem.

113. The army of the crusaders.

114. Likely a valley between Gaza and Rama.

115. That is, Gaston of Béarn.

116. This refers to the various pilgrims that came to Jerusalem in the years well before the First Crusade.

117. That is, Cairo.

118. A silver value equal to one silver pound.

119. Friday, August 12, 1099.

DESCRIPTION OF THE HOLY PLACES OF JERUSALEM

1. An apocryphal book of the Bible.

2. Matthew 23:35 (so that upon you may fall the guilt of all the righteous blood shed on earth, from the blood of righteous Abel to the blood of

Zechariah, the son of Berechiah, whom you murdered between the temple and the altar).

3. Cf. Exodus 30:26 (Moreover, the Lord spoke to Moses, saying, "Take also for yourself the finest of spices: of flowing myrrh five hundred shekels, and of fragrant cinnamon half as much, two hundred and fifty, and of fragrant cane two hundred and fifty, and of cassia five hundred, according to the shekel of the sanctuary, and of olive oil a hin. You shall make of these a holy anointing oil, a perfume mixture, the work of a perfumer; it shall be a holy anointing oil. With it you shall anoint the tent of meeting and the ark of the testimony").

4. 2 Kings 20:6 (I will add fifteen years to your life, and I will deliver you and this city from the hand of the king of Assyria; and I will defend this city for My own sake and for My servant David's sake).

5. This is, of course, the Church of the Holy Sepulcher, which Constantine the Great had constructed around 326 AD.

6. John 19:26–27 (When Jesus saw his mother and the disciple whom he loved standing nearby, he said to his mother, "Woman, behold, your son!" Then he said to the disciple, "Behold, your mother!" And from that hour the disciple took her to his own home).

7. This is Simeon the Righteous. See Luke 2:25–35.

8. This is the Pool of Bethesda, or the Sheep Pool, where crusaders eventually built a church.

9. Matthew 26:39 (And going a little farther he fell on his face and prayed, saying, "My Father, if it be possible, let this cup pass from me; nevertheless, not as I will, but as you will").

10. Matthew 28:19 (Go therefore and make disciples of all nations, baptizing them in the name of the Father and of the Son and of the Holy Spirit).

MASS IN VENERATION OF THE HOLY SEPULCHER

1. This line represents the height of Jesus Christ, which comes to 6'4".

2. This line measures the width of Christ's body, which comes to 2'11".

VERSE IN PRAISE OF BOHEMOND

1. This verse appears at the end of the Vatican manuscript *Reginensis latini 572*, and given its connection to Bohemond, the leader of the Normans from southern Italy during the First Crusade, it is included here.

FOUR NAMES

1. This list of four names appears at the end of the Vatican manuscript *Reginensis latini 641*. Since the handwriting is from the twelfth century, from the time of the *Gesta*, they are included here. Perhaps they are the "authors" of the *Gesta*?

Selected Bibliography

PRIMARY SOURCES

Jacques Bongars. Ed. *Gesta Dei per Francos*. Hanover, Aubrius, 1611.

Louis Bréhier. Ed. *Histoire anonyme de la première croisade*. Paris: H. Champion, 1924.

Heinrich Hagenmeyer. Ed. *Anonymi Gesta Francorum et aliorum Hierosolymitanorum*. Heidelberg: C. Winter, 1890.

Rosalind Hill. Ed. and Trans. *The Deeds of the Franks and the Other Pilgrims to Jerusalem*. Oxford: Clarendon Press, 1979.

P. Le Bas. Ed. *Recueil des historiens des croisades: Historiens occidentaux*. Vol. 3. Paris: l'Académie royale, 1866, pp. 121–163.

FURTHER READING

Thomas Asbridge. *The First Crusade: A New History*. London; New York: Free Press, 2004.

Marcus Bull, Norman Housley, Peter Edbury, and Jonathan Phillips. Eds. 2 vols. *The Experience of Crusading*. Cambridge: Cambridge University Press, 2003.

Marcus Graham Bull. *Knightly Piety and the Lay Response to the First Crusade: The Limousin and Gascony, c. 970–c. 1130*. Oxford: Clarendon Press; New York: Oxford University Press, 1993.

———. *Thinking Medieval: An Introduction to the Study of the Middle Ages*. Basingstoke: Palgrave Macmillan, 2005.

Robert Chazan. *In the Year 1096: The First Crusade and the Jews.* Philadelphia: Jewish Publication Society, 1996.

Susan B. Edgington. *The First Crusade.* London: Historical Association, 1996.

Jean Flori. *La Première Croisade: L'Occident chrétien contre l'Islam.* Paris: Editions Complexe, 1992.

John France. *Victory in the East: A Military History of the First Crusade.* Cambridge: Cambridge University Press, 1994.

Jacques Heers. *Libérer Jérusalem: La Première Croisade, 1095–1107.* Paris: Perrin, 1995.

Conor Kostick. *The Social Structure of the First Crusade.* Leiden; Boston: Brill, 2008.

———. *The Siege of Jerusalem: Crusade and Conquest in 1099.* London; New York: Continuum, 2009.

August C. Krey. *The First Crusade. The Accounts of Eye-Witnesses and Participants.* Princeton: Princeton University Press, 1921.

Thomas F. Madden. Ed. *The Crusades: The Essential Readings.* Oxford, UK; Malden, MA: Blackwell, 2002.

Thomas F. Madden and Peter Bently. Eds. *Crusades: The Illustrated History.* London: Duncan Baird, 2004.

Paul Magdalino. *The Byzantine Background to the First Crusade.* Toronto: Canadian Institute of Balkan Studies, 1996.

Alan V. Murray. Ed. *From Clermont to Jerusalem: The Crusades and Crusader Societies, 1095–1500.* Turnhout: Brepols, 1998.

Geoffrey Regan. *First Crusader: Byzantium's Holy Wars.* Stroud: Sutton, 2001.

Susan J. Ridyard. Ed. *The Medieval Crusade.* Woodbridge, Suffolk; Rochester, NY: Boydell Press, 2004.

Jonathan Riley-Smith. *The First Crusade and the Idea of Crusading.* London: Athlone Press, 1986.

———. *The First Crusaders, 1095–1131.* Cambridge: Cambridge University Press, 1997.

Steven Runciman. *The First Crusade.* Cambridge; New York: Cambridge University Press, 1980.

Maya Shatzmiller. Ed. *Crusaders and Muslims in Twelfth-Century Syria.* Leiden: Brill, 1993.

Index